COWBOY

Books by Daniel Ford

Flying Tigers: Claire Chennault and His American Volunteers, 1941-1942

Tales of the Flying Tigers

Poland's Daughter: How I Met Basia, Hitchhiked to Italy, and Learned About Love, War, and Exile

A Vision So Noble: John Boyd, the OODA Loop, and America's War on Terror

The Lady and the Tigers (with Olga Greenlaw)

Glen Edwards: The Diary of a Bomber Pilot

The Only War We've Got: Early Days in South Vietnam

The Country Northward: A Hiker's Journal

Fiction

Michael's War: A Story of the Irish Republican Army

Remains: A Story of the Flying Tigers

The High Country Illuminator: A Tale of Light and Darkness and the Ski Bums of Avalon

Incident at Muc Wa: A Story of the Vietnam War

Now Comes Theodora: A College Novel

Thank you for your interest. For more about the author and his work, or to sign up for his monthly electronic newsletter, visit his website at danfordbooks.com

COWBOY

*The Interpreter Who
Became a Soldier,
a Warlord, and One
More Casualty of
Our War in Vietnam*

Daniel Ford

Warbird Books
Durham, New Hampshire, USA
2018

ISBN 978-1-7322300-0-2

Library of Congress Control Number: 2018904385

Contents

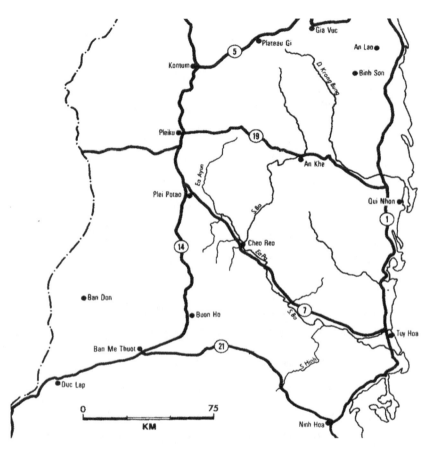

Heart of the Highlands: From north to south, the population centers in the Highlands were Kontum, Pleiku, Cheo Reo, and Ban Me Thuot. The last would be crucial to Cowboy's life story, to Hanoi's strategy for conquering South Vietnam, and to the survival of the Saigon regime. (US government)

The Invention of Philippe Drouin

FOR A VISITOR to the Highlands in 1964, South Vietnam's most famous citizen wasn't the current strongman in Saigon, and certainly not the province chief, but a flamboyant interpreter who called himself Cowboy. He was an "Asian version of the Marlboro Man," in the words of Johnnie Corns, then a captain in the US Army Special Forces, the Green Berets of song and story.

I met Cowboy that June, and one of the sorrows of my life is that I didn't take the time to photograph him as an individual. Now, the best I can do is crop him out of a scenic photo of a Strike Force company, marching to evacuate the village of Tan Hoa. We'd been told to move its population to safety in a Strategic Hamlet, so the region could become a free-fire zone, where anything that moved could be bombed, shelled, or shot. But when we reached Tan Hoa, it had no houses and no residents, just a French graveyard and some foxholes dating back to the First Indochina War.

I have used that image of Cowboy on the cover of this book. I hope it suggests how handsome he was, and how wonderfully well he carried himself. I've since found a few other pictures of him, which I include in *Portfolio: The Strikers at War*, starting on page 93.

In memory, he seems about my own height. In reality, he was much shorter: "a three-fifth scale model

1

of a Choctaw Indian," in the words of Jim Morris, another Green Beret whom he served as interpreter, friend, and bodyguard. Judging by photos of Cowboy standing next to an American of known height, he was about five foot five.

And his fame outlived him. I recently exchanged emails with Carter Carr, whose first post in Vietnam was the Thuong Duc Camp near Danang. Far to the north of Philippe's area of operations, and more than a year after he was executed, the story of the enterprising interpreter was well known at Thuong Duc. "Almost everybody in Special Forces knew or had heard about Cowboy," Carter assured me.

Philippe lived a life as dramatic as it was short, lasting as it did from 1936 to 1968. He was born into the Rhade, one of fifty-odd mountain tribes that have inhabited the Highlands for thousands of years. The lowland Vietnamese — relative newcomers to the southern half of the country — dismissed them as *moi*, or savages, and shunned both them and the land they inhabited.

The French, who colonized what they called Indochina (now Vietnam, Cambodia, and Laos) in the 1850s, had a different view. They regarded the Highlanders as able and useful — "the *mois* more and more furnish us regularly with strong and honest labor," wrote the colonial governor in 1902 — and in time dignified them with the name of *Montagnards*, or mountaineers. This eventually became the accepted term among foreigners, though American soldiers — of course! — would shorten it to "Yards."

Working for the French was obligatory, typically ten days a year for Highland men between the ages of eighteen and fifty-five. For a day's labor, they earned ten centimes, about thirty-five US cents today, so it seems more slave than honest labor.

French missionaries moved into the Highlands to save souls, French planters to grow coffee and rubber trees, and French soldiers to protect them. In time, military garrisons became administrative centers, and footpaths became rough roads. Out of this activity, towns grew in the early years of the twentieth century: Kontum, Pleiku, Cheo Reo, Ban Me Thuot, and Dalat, ranged from north to south. Highland families lived together in communities of ten to a hundred long-houses; even after the garrisons grew into substantial settlements, the center was given over to a French quarter and a foreign quarter, with the latter home to Vietnamese and Chinese merchants. The *moi* or *Montagnards* lived in village clusters on the periphery.

In 1943, when the French conducted a census, they counted about one million Highlanders but only 42,267 Vietnamese living in the mountainous regions, along with 5,090 French planters, soldiers, administrators, and missionaries. Of the native population, the Jarai were the most numerous at about 150,000, followed by the Bahnar with 80,000 and the Rhade with 60,000.

~ ~ ~

Under whatever name, the Highlanders got along better with the foreigners than either did with the lowland Vietnamese. And of all the tribes, the Rhade seemed especially promising as soldiers, clerks, teachers, and minor bureaucrats. Many became Christians, whether Catholic because of the French influence, or Protestant from the preaching of American missionaries. In time, indeed, Rhade became something of a universal language for doing business in the Highlands. It helped that the scores of tribal languages fell into two major groups, and that some were closely related — like Spanish and Portuguese, say, or even the regional dialects of Italy.

For the Rhade, descent ran through the female line. Philippe's mother was a Mlo and apparently of high status. She lived in the village of Buon Pan Lam on the outskirts of Ban Me Thuot, the capital of Darlac province. (The name means the "Village of Thuot's Father.") With about 140,000 Rhade, Vietnamese, and Chinese residents, in the built-up area and surrounding villages, it was one of five significant population centers in the Highlands.

The boy's father is sometimes identified as a Javanese migrant worker, employed by the French to build a road system through the Highlands. The Rhade, because they organized families around the women, worried little about paternity. Ordinarily a girl would marry the lad who fathered her child, but that option wasn't available to the boy's mother. It made little practical difference: a Rhade baby took the family name of its mother. The boy became Y Kdruin Mlo, identifying him as the male descendant (the prefix *Y*) of the Mlo family, with the personal name of Kdruin. His eventual stepfather was a driver for Bao Dai, the last emperor of Vietnam and later a figurehead ruler for the French, who had build an elaborate hunting lodge in Ban Me Thuot, along with a "Grand Bungalow" for his guests.

By all accounts, Y Kdruin had a privileged upbringing, despite the war that was savaging Asia. In

May 1940, when he was four, the German army conquered France, which enabled the Japanese to seize the northern half of Vietnam, the better to prosecute their long-running rape of China. In 1941, they moved into southern Vietnam and Cambodia, as a base from which to attack the British in Malaya and the Dutch in Indonesia. But like the ethnic Vietnamese, the Japanese concerned themselves mostly with the cities and the seacoast, leaving the French Colonial Army to manage the hinterland.

Y Kdruin was nine when Japan surrendered in 1945. The French promptly returned to Saigon and regained control over the southern half of the country. In the north, however, the Chinese took over, which enabled the rise of the man whom the world would know as Ho Chi Minh. Born in Hoang Tru in northern Vietnam, he spent most of his early life in exile, including a stint at the Lenin Institute in Moscow, where he trained as a Soviet agent. He next appeared in China as an advisor to Mao's Red Army, during which time he adopted the name by which he would become famous. As Ho Chi Minh, he returned to Vietnam in 1941 and raised a revolutionary army called the Viet Minh, which nibbled without much effect at both the French and the Japanese. He was supported in this by American agents of the Office of Strategic Services, forerunner of the Central Intelligence Agency, based in China. (Against Vietnamese custom, he seems never to have been known as "Minh," but by his first name or indeed as "Uncle Ho." For more about Vietnamese names, see the chapter notes, beginning on page 144.)

On August 25, 1945, ten days after Japan's surrender, Ho proclaimed the Democratic Republic of Vietnam with its capital at Hanoi. (One story has him riding into the city on an OSS jeep.) The DRVN was the first Communist government not to have a common border with the Soviet Union, and it was recognized by no other government at the time, not even by Moscow.

Over the next few years, the struggle between the French Colonial Army and the Viet Minh escalated from skirmishes to set-piece battles. It soon became a proxy for the Cold War that had set the victors of the Second World War against one another, the US-dominated West against the Soviet-dominated East, which after 1949 included the People's Republic of China. The Chinese supplied and supported the Viet Minh; the Americans supplied and supported the French. Thus began the First Indochina War.

In the comparative peace of the Highlands, Y Kdruin Mlo graduated from the *Groupe Scholaire Antomarchi*, a six-year elementary school in Ban Me Thuot, one of several established by the French to educate young Highlanders who might serve in the military or the civil government. He went on to attend the *Collège Sabatier*, a two-year secondary school established in 1947 to foster a friendly elite among the Rhade, the Jarai, and other Highland tribes. This cross-cultural mingling would in time lead to marriages between the tribes, and to the Rhade language becoming widely spoken across the Highlands.

His classmates remembered Philippe (as he now styled himself) racing about on a motorbike, an almost unheard-of luxury at that time and place. "He was a spoiled kid," one schoolmate later said of him,

6

adding that he regularly got into fights with the other boys.

But he seems to have learned! Fluent in French, and speaking at least some Vietnamese, he graduated as Philippe Drouin, and under that name joined the French Colonial Army, probably in a Highland regiment. He was lucky enough to be stationed in Cambodia, where King Norodom Sihanouk was negotiating his country's independence from France while also playing along with Ho Chi Minh's Communists. One of his tools in this campaign was a cross-border organization called the *Front de Libération des Hauts-Plateaux* (Front for the Liberation of the High Country). The FLHP was meant to unite his Cham and Khmer Highlanders with those across the border in Vietnam, thus increasing his leverage against the French.

Philippe's stepfather managed to bring him home before his enlistment was up, but apparently not before the teenager had become a Highland nationalist in his own right. Mingling with lads of other tribal origins, first in high school and then in the army, he began to think of himself first as a Highlander and only secondarily as a member of the Rhade community. And, like most mountain tribesmen, he didn't think of himself at all as Vietnamese.

~ ~ ~

In 1953, when Philippe was seventeen, the French gave in to Norodom Sihanouk and set Cambodia free. A year later, they gave up their attempt to control Vietnam, following a calamitous defeat in the valley of Dien Bien Phu in May 1954. That disaster, combined with a new colonial revolt in Algeria, sent them to the bargaining table. At a peace conference in Switzerland, they agreed to divide Indochina into its four more or less historic parts, with national governments in Cambodia, Laos, North Vietnam (presided over by Ho Chi Minh), and South Vietnam (under the former emperor Bao Dai, who increasingly would be dominated by his prime minister, Ngo Dinh Diem).

Under the Geneva Accords, the two Vietnams were policed by a United Nations peacekeeping force of Indian, Polish, and Canadian soldiers, pending an election to unify the country under a mutually acceptable government. It was a farce, like so many UN endeavors. In Saigon ten years later, I was assured that whenever a shooting occurred, the Eastern Bloc Pole would blame the South Vietnamese, the Western Bloc Canadian would blame the Communists, and the non-aligned Indian just shrugged his shoulders. It scarcely mattered, since the US or the USSR would veto any finding that hurt its proxy. Despite the futility, the "peacekeepers" would stay on the job for nearly twenty years.

The last French soldiers left Vietnam in 1956. As the story is told, when the troops marched up the gangway at the port of Haiphong, the song they sang was "Lili Marlene." There were that many Germans in the Foreign Legion.

They were soon replaced by American military and civilian advisory teams. Neither the Saigon government nor the Americans had any interest in an election that would probably result in a larger Communist nation. Nor did Ho Chi Minh have any intention of compromising his plan for total control of what he regarded as his country.

8

More than a million North Vietnamese – most of them Catholics, businessmen, and those with connections to the French – came south after the partition. The Saigon government began to settle many of them in the Highlands, especially on land the Rhade and Bahnar regarded as their own. The two tribes were alarmed enough to establish the *Front Pour la Libération des Montagnards*, Front for the Liberation of the Highland People. The site was Ban Me Thuot, and more specifically the village of Buon Ale A, on Route 14 south of the built-up area. (The ubiquitous "buon" or "ban" was a Rhade term for a small community.) Buon Ale A seemed to attract outsiders. Here Bao Dai had built his hunting lodge and Grand Bungalow, and here too was the home of the American Christian and Missionary Alliance.

In 1958, representatives of the Jarai and the Kaho were brought into the movement, which became the *Bajaraka*, representing the names of all four tribes. The organization was headed by Y Bham Enoul, a Rhade who had been an administrator in the colonial agriculture service. Another leader was Paul Nur, whose mother was Bahnar and his father part Vietnamese. Both men were Christians. Finally, there was Nay Luett, a Jarai who has been described as "a Montagnard educated in France and speaking six languages." The first is unlikely, but the second seems true enough. Mike Benge, who worked for the Agency for International Development (USAID) in Ban Me Thuot, recalled that Nay Luett spoke French, English, Vietnamese, Jarai, Rhade, and at least one other tribal language.

Y Bham believed that Bajaraka could use peaceful

means to persuade the Diem regime to moderate its resettlement program. But after demonstrations in Kontum, Pleiku, and Ban Me Thuot, where two thousand Highlanders came out to demand their right to self-government, the Saigon government stupidly jailed Y Bham, Paul Nur, Nay Luett, and other leaders. Worse, the government seized the Highlanders' spears and crossbows, which not only left them defenseless but unable to hunt for meat. Predictably, that encouraged the rise of a more militant group, led by Y Dhon Adrong, who had been Philippe's classmate at the Collège Sabatier. Another discontented Rhade opted to join the left-behind Communist guerrillas, who put him in charge of their efforts to recruit among the Highlanders.

Y Dhon and his followers moved across the border to a former French fort, Camp le Rolland, which today is the Cambodian town of Phumi Dak Dam. Fittingly enough, the post had been created in 1932 by a Rhade company of the French Colonial Army, assigned to protect the men working on Route 14, intended as a north-south highway connecting Ban Me Thuot with Saigon. At Camp le Rolland, the militants established a military base and a new organization, joining the Bajaraka tribes with the Sihanouk-inspired FLHP, which was represented by two Cambodian army officers.

The new group would eventually call itself the *Front Unifié de Lutte des Races Opprimées*, United Fighting Front for the Liberation of Oppressed Races. FULRO even had its own flag, with stripes of blue, red, and green, overlaid with white stars to represent the Highlanders of Vietnam and the Cham and Khmer people of Cambodia.

~ ~ ~

At this time, the Army of the Republic of [South] Vietnam — the ARVN — was training to repel an invasion across the 17th Parallel, like the one that had launched the Korean War in 1950. The Vietnamese were of course encouraged in this by their American advisors, who'd been obliged to fight that seesaw and ultimately stalemated battle. As a result, the ARVN tended to ignore the "dirty war" being waged in the countryside by left-behind and infiltrated Communists. The latter would give themselves the title of National Liberation Front, but Saigon preferred the less flattering term Viet Cong, which Americans rendered as VC — "Victor Charlie," in the phonetic alphabet.

While the ARVN prepared to repel a conventional invasion, the guerrillas were left to ragtag militias whose names were translated as Regional Forces and Popular Forces, which the Americans lumped together as the "Ruff Puffs."

In 1956, the VC began to wage a relentless murder campaign to rid the South Vietnamese countryside of teachers, village officials, policemen, landlords, and anyone else who represented the Saigon regime. Armed skirmishes, such as they were, were mostly intended to capture weapons and discourage government forces from traveling the roads at night; they generally left the ARVN alone. By 1961, however, this was beginning to change. Increasingly, the VC were being supplied and reinforced by the People's Army of [North] Vietnam, the PAVN, over a trail system that bypassed the demilitarized zone at the 17th Parallel and wound through the back country of Laos and Cambodia. Americans would come to know this route as the Ho Chi Minh Trail.

I find no mention of Philippe Drouin in these years, from the time he left the French Colonial Army to the day he turned up at Buon Enao, a Rhade village a few kilometers east of Ban Me Thuot, the heart of the Vietnamese Highlands.

Dave Nuttle and the CIA

THE HIGHLANDS are rugged, vast in area, and scarce in population, and they extend across Vietnam's western frontier into Cambodia and Laos. For all these reasons, they became the key to Hanoi's strategy for extending Communism's reach. They provided an infiltration route through supposedly neutral countries, forests to hide in while they trained or regrouped within South Vietnam, and the ability to concentrate a superior force on an isolated outpost — then ambush the relief column sent to rescue the defenders.

And if they could dominate the Highlands, the Communists would be in a position to march to the South China Sea and cut South Vietnam in half. They thought they could accomplish this by 1963, but in fact it would require twelve more years, two or three million lives, and something close to a revolution in the United States.

Saigon's plan to head off this threat could have been modeled on what the United States had done to native Americans in the nineteenth century: it would herd the aborigines onto "reservations." The French had started an *agroville* program in 1952, and Ngo Dinh Diem copied it in 1959, neither with any success. By the spring of 1961, the Americans decided to bring their know-how to the problem. William Colby, the Central Intelligence Agency chief in Saigon, and

Gilbert Layton, a retired Army officer responsible for CIA military operations in the country, began to look for a better way to reduce the VC threat in the Highlands.

As it happened, Colonel Layton knew an American civilian who lived and worked in Ban Me Thuot. This was David Nuttle, a stocky 25-year-old who had grown up on a Kansas ranch during the Second World War. Like many country boys of the time, Dave hunted small game, ran a trap-line for pelts, and worked on the family ranch. "Self-sufficiency was always a priority [in] my family," he wrote in later years, "and we grew and preserved all the food crops [we] needed and reared our own pork, beef, and chicken."

Dave studied animal science at Kansas State University, graduating in 1958 from its ROTC program and afterward joining the Air National Guard, which put him on inactive duty. (The Korean War was long finished, and Vietnam did not yet require an influx of second lieutenants.) This allowed him to join the International Voluntary Service, the IVS, a Quaker-affiliated predecessor to the Peace Corps. His first assignment was to help resettle those refugees from North Vietnam. He next joined the staff of an agricultural experiment station at Ea Kmat, near Ban Me Thuot, where he helped its mostly Vietnamese staff develop a fiber industry and introduce the Highlanders to improved hand tools, water conservation, and organic farming.

Unusual for an American, Dave set out to learn the language and mores of the Rhade. He bought a small BMW motorcycle and made a friend of Y Rit, an interpreter for the Christian and Missionary Alliance in Buon Ale A whom Dave was able to hire as his counterpart at the experiment station. Together they traveled to outlying villages, talking to their leaders and working with them to solve their problems, including their government-imposed lack of weapons for hunting.

"Many nights," Dave wrote of his time in Vietnam, "I would go with tribal hunting parties to use my rifle to harvest game from the jungle so villagers would have fresh meat." He shot deer, wild pigs, and the occasional tiger, using a bolt-action Winchester Model 70 bought from a US Army major. The Model 70 is a formidable weapon, firing the .375 Magnum bullet favored by hunters of large or dangerous game. (The caliber of a bullet is its diameter in inches, with .375 equaling 9.5 mm.) It had a correspondingly fierce recoil, which had proved too much for the American officer.

Though one Kansan with one rifle could supply meat to the Rhade, he couldn't protect them from the Viet Cong guerrillas who by this time controlled much of the countryside. They harassed the outlying villages, demanding food and conscripting young men as laborers or guerrillas. Worse, the ARVN response was often to shell any village that came under Communist control, or to call for the air force to bomb and strafe it. "The Montagnard were being trampled by opposing armed forces," Dave recalled, with both the government and the Viet Cong "seeking to end what each perceived as Montagnard support for their enemy."

Dave was a regular visitor to Saigon, sometimes covering the 350 kilometers on his BMW motorcycle, the better to pursue an acquaintance with a young woman who happened to be Colonel Layton's daughter. Layton and Colby by this time — April 1961 — had settled on a two-pronged strategy to quell the VC in the countryside. First, they would bring in some Green Berets to train small teams of "Mountain Scouts" to find the VC, kill their leaders, poison or burn their rice stores, and otherwise turn their guerrilla tactics against them.

The second prong would be the Citizen's Irregular Defense Group. With a trivial investment in time, money, and weapons, a village could be fenced, some of its men armed and trained, and the Viet Cong kept away. Seeing their neighbors gain in security and government services, nearby villages would ask to join the program, and soon an entire region would be secure. (Later, "citizens" became "civilian." The terms were alike misleading, since the CIDG troops were paid a small salary and subject to military discipline.)

In his daughter's boyfriend, Layton saw the tool to get the CIDG started. Or perhaps, as Dave Nuttle remembers the circumstances, the situation was reversed and he was the one who came up with the idea. However it happened, Layton shopped the concept to Bill Colby, who in turn presented it to Ambassador Frederick Nolting and then to President Diem's influential brother, Ngo Dinh Nhu. In July, the ambassador called a meeting of his "country team," including Colby and his US Army equivalent, Lieutenant General Lionel McGarr, head of the Military Assistance Advisory Group for Vietnam.

16

The agenda was to explore ways "to stop a possible VC takeover of the Highlands." It seems to have been stage-managed, with Dave Nuttle there to present the case against a purely military solution. Like the French before them, the US military wanted to force the people into large, fortified settlements, so the fields and forest could become a free-fire zone for the ARVN and the Vietnamese air force. As expected, General McGarr made the case for what would in time be known as Strategic Hamlets.

On cue, Dave objected. The Highlanders could easily escape to the forest, he pointed out, and their survival skills would make them almost impossible to recapture. Sooner or later, they would come under VC control.

Well, huffed General McGarr, that might be true, but what was the alternative? That was Colby's cue to ask for suggestions, whereupon Dave outlined the notion of training and arming Highlanders in their own villages. They cared nothing about the Saigon regime, he argued, but they would "fight to defend family, home and village." In so doing, they would aid the government "by resisting VC control, taxation and conscription of young men."

Ambassador Nolting chimed in: would Nuttle be willing to set up a demonstration project?

"I said yes," Dave recalled, "and Colby quickly said CIA will support such an attempt as needed." In the early years, the CIA and not the US military was responsible for Special Forces operations in South Vietnam, so this would make the village defense program independent of General McGarr and the US Army advisory mission.

Of course the proposal had to filter through the Diem family, the ARVN, and the province chief in Ban Me Thuot. By the first week of October 1961, everything was in place. Dave resigned from the IVS, Bill Colby hired him for the CIA, and the pair of them visited Ngo Dinh Nhu to hear the conditions. The president's brother agreed that crossbows and spears would be returned to the men in the test village, and they in turn must fence the village, swear allegiance to the Saigon government, and threaten death to any VC who entered. That done, he would let them have firearms and military training.

And the scheme had to be approved by Washington as well. On October 26, CIA chief Allen Dulles signed off on Saigon's proposal for a Village Defense program in the Highlands.

Special Forces teams had been in the country since the 1950s, training the *Loc Luong Dac Biet* as their counterparts, though in practice the LLDB avoided combat and spent most of their time suppressing Diem's internal enemies. The Americans liked to render the Vietnamese name as "Look long, duck back," said very quickly.

From the LLDB training center in the old imperial capital of Hue, Colby detached an American Green Beret, Sergeant Paul Campbell, trained as a medic. For two weeks in October, he and Dave Nuttle visited twenty-two Rhade villages in a sixty-kilometer radius. While "Doctor Paul" held a sick call for the villagers,

"Mister Dave" chatted with the village elders, sounding out their attitude toward the government and their openness to a self-defense program.

At five foot five and one hundred thirty pounds, Campbell was ideal for working with the Rhade, whose stature was not all that different from his. Like Dave Nuttle, he wore civilian clothes and carried no weapon. In his first sick call, indeed, he presented himself as an assistant to the village shaman, so the wise man wouldn't lose face when the foreigner's medicine cured a child of dysentery.

To launch the experiment, Dave Nuttle chose Buon Enao, where the headman, Y Ju, was already an old friend. To provide military training and protect the village until firearms were distributed, Nhu sent a team from the Loc Luong Dac Biet. Remarkably, it was made up entirely of Rhade and Jarai tribesmen, including the commander, Captain Khoai, a native of Darlac province. His was one of only two Highlander teams in the LLDB, and this seems to have been the first time that a team was used for the purpose for which the Green Berets had trained them.

Captain Khoai and his men recruited a thirty-man Village Defense force and led them on patrols and ambushes, armed only with crossbows and spears. Unlike the ethnic Vietnamese who staffed later LLDB teams in the Highlands, they worked easily with the volunteers and treated them with respect. "Capt. Khoai was a great project asset," Dave Nuttle said.

Meanwhile, a swarm of workers surrounded Buon Enao with inner and outer fences of bamboo, with the

19

space between them bristling with *punji* sticks. (A punji was a spike planted in the ground, sharpened at the upper end, and the tip poisoned or contaminated with excrement. Deployed by both sides during the Vietnam War, it inflicted nasty foot wounds.) For a day's work on the defenses, they were paid thirty-five piasters. At the black-market exchange of the 1960s, a piaster was worth about one US cent, while a 1961 penny equates to one of our dimes, so call the stipend $3.50.

Some of the men in the construction crew were refugees from villages that had been overrun by the VC and, as a result, been destroyed by ARVN artillery. Comically, but in all seriousness, Bill Colby remarked that "some of our Rhade have been treated as bad or worse by the Viet Cong as by the government."

Sergeant Campbell supervised the construction of a dispensary and trained four young Rhade women as medics to staff it. (The medics earned 900 piasters a month, worth about $90 today.) In December, however, he came down with hepatitis and had to fly back to Okinawa for treatment. He was replaced by Dr. Dun Ksor, a rare Highlander who had graduated from medical school; under his direction, the dispensary would evolve into a fairly sophisticated field hospital, "even performing amputations," as the military historian Paul Harris tells us, "and doing so with great competence."

With the fence in place, an anti-VC sign over the gate, and the South Vietnamese flag duly displayed, Ngo Dinh Nhu made good on his promise that the village defenders could carry firearms. No one came forward to supply them, however, so the CIA in Saigon absconded with fifty US Army carbines from a delivery that were supposed to have gone to the ARVN. And on December 12, six US Army Special Forces arrived to help the LLDB with firearms training and to develop a semi-professional militia whose members would be paid a small daily wage — the beginnings of the CIDG envisioned by Gilbert Layton. Like Sergeant Campbell, the new Green Berets wore civilian clothes when they worked with the Highlanders.

The newcomers were led by Captain Lawrence Arritola, a bespectacled young man with a buzz haircut. He was the executive officer — the second in command — of Detachment A-213. Splitting a detachment was not unusual in the early years of Special Forces in Vietnam. In this case, the commanding officer and five noncoms (non-commissioned officers, usually a sergeant or a specialist) went north to Danang to help train the first Mountain Scouts, the hunter-killer teams that would later become the CIA's Phoenix Program. It seemed a choice assignment, but they paid a high price for it: the commander would be killed in January 1962, and two noncoms were later captured and murdered by the Viet Cong because they were too wounded to keep up with the guerrillas.

Finally, and more to the point for this story, Philippe Drouin signed on. He was twenty-five by this time, the same age as Dave Nuttle, who hired him as a truck driver. He proved to be a quick study. Soon he was working with the Americans as an interpreter — he was fluent in Rhade, of course, and he could speak Vietnamese if it was necessary to communicate with the ARVN or the province chief in Ban Me Thuot. He also had a fair command of English, though he needed a while to master American military nomenclature. In time, indeed, he was helping to train the Village Defenders. "In brief," as Dave Nuttle explains in an email, "he had two jobs at Buon Enao and was good at both."

A Special Forces account of the Buon Enao project lists the weapons it received during the first half of 1962: 1,060 M-1 carbines of Second World War vintage, 1,950 Springfield rifles dating back to the First World War, 1,840 fairly modern Danish and Swedish sub-machineguns, and about 450 machineguns, pistols, shotguns, and other weaponry. From what was available when he joined, Philippe chose a "Swedish K" as his personal firearm.

The "K" was a cheap, reliable sub-machinegun adopted by the Swedish army in 1945. It had a folding stock and a magazine holding thirty-six 9 mm bullets. When I traveled around Vietnam, the "K" was highly prized by helicopter crews, who traded for it when we visited Special Forces camps. The Green Berets had acquired it in quantity during the years they served under the CIA in Vietnam. It weighed no more than a standard infantry rifle, was fairly accurate at close quarters, and kept firing when dirty and wet — great virtues in a jungle war. It had no semi-automatic setting, but a well-trained soldier could easily squeeze off single shots and thereby conserve ammunition and improve his chances of hitting his target.

That Philippe chose the "K" as his personal firearm suggests that, though he might have been a bit shaky about military nomenclature, he could recognize the ideal weapon when he saw it.

The Rise and Fall of Buon Enao

CAPTAIN ARRITOLA and his men had their work cut out for them. When I toured the Highlands in June of 1964, I was often told that the "Yards" were natural warriors. All a Green Beret needed to do, it seemed, was give a tribesman an M-1 carbine and turn him loose on the Viet Cong. That was far from the case, as Gilbert Layton remembered the early days at Buon Enao. The Village Defenders, he recalled in a 1991 interview, were so terrified of the VC that the first time a patrol encountered one in the field, the militiamen froze. Only after the guerrilla was shot and killed by a Special Forces sergeant did they snap out of their trance, run up to the dead man, and riddle his body with bullets. Only then did the VC lose their aura of invincibility.

The Americans also worried that some of their recruits might be Communist infiltrators or sympathizers. Accordingly, after a firefight or a hunt for game, the Highlanders were told to retrieve the shells that had been ejected from their weapons. With an allowance for "brass" that couldn't be found, this enabled a close inventory of the CIDG ordnance, to ensure that no one was passing ammunition along to the guerrillas.

Meanwhile, neighboring villages were lured into

24

the project. The medics trained by Paul Campbell would hold a sick call for the residents, to introduce them to the wonders of aspirin and iodine and — especially treasured by the Highlanders — adhesive bandages. An "information team" followed up with entertainment, propaganda, and low-key espionage. As Dave Nuttle had expected and Gilbert Layton had hoped, other villages soon began asking to join the program, so they could get their own defense force and enjoy medical care, the occasional movie, and a radio to call for help if they were attacked.

The growth rate was astonishing. In the first six months, forty villages signed up. Each built a security fence, swore loyalty to the Saigon government, and provided twenty or thirty volunteer militiamen. Altogether, fourteen thousand Highlanders were in secure communities by the spring of 1962, defended by 975 volunteer militiamen. If needed, they could call on a Strike Force company of 120 men, based at Buon Enao or an area development center. I can't discover who named the Strikers, but Buon Enao in 1961-1962 does seem to be the first time that the term was used to describe a quick-reaction military unit.

To start, most of the villages were Rhade, but the Jarai and Mnong became interested as well. And one Jarai is particularly worth mentioning: Rcom H'un, a chief's daughter from Cheo Reo, 120 kilometers to the north. Like Philippe Drouin, H'un came from the Highlander elite. Americans sometimes described her as a "Jarai princess" with a French grandfather, just as they liked to think of Philippe as the son of a mythic

"Captain Drouin," veteran of the lost battle of Dien Bien Phu.

It's true that the Rcom clan was prestigious. The "King of Water," a principal Highlander shaman, was usually the son of an Rcom woman. But as the anthropologist Gerald Hickey wrote of the early French travelers, their awe at these royalties diminished when they realized that the kings "wore loinclothes and lived in ordinary houses" like their followers.

By all accounts, H'un was a beautiful woman, with pale tawny skin and long, curly hair, shot through with red. As a chief's daughter, she wore traditional Highland dress. Dave Nuttle, in his unpublished memoir, described her as "the very attractive and intelligent eighteen-year-old daughter of Nay Moul, supreme chief of the Jarai."

He was indeed a chief, but for the Jarai (and the Rhade as well) it was the wife who determined how the family organized itself. The earlier chief was Nay Nui, whose marriage to an Rcom woman was so successful that everyone agreed that the clans should again be brought together. He married off one of his daughters to the Cheo Reo schoolmaster and another to Nay Moul, who had distinguished himself as an athlete and a junior officer in the French Colonial Army. (He also served briefly as a Viet Minh rebel.) Moreover, his bearing seemed to qualify him to become chief in his turn.

So it was Nay Moul who moved into the family longhouse with his wife, Rcom H'ban, along with her parents while they still lived, with her married sisters, and with those of their daughters who got married, each couple in its own compartment. There were communal rooms for the unmarried children.

Perhaps significantly, one married daughter was Rcom H'chem, the wife of Nay Luett, imprisoned in 1958 by the Diem regime. So this Highlander rebel was H'un's brother-in-law. This connection might well have had something to do with her interest in Dave Nuttle.

They'd met when Dave was an IVS volunteer at the Ea Kmat agricultural experiment station. They hit it off from the beginning, but the attraction became serious in the winter of 1961-62 when H'un came to see him at Buon Enao, hoping that the defense program could be applied to her own village near Cheo Reo. (Gilbert Layton's daughter had gone back to the United States by this time.) It was H'un who proposed marriage, as was the custom among the matrilineal Jarai.

Tradition also called for a husband to reside with his wife's family, which wasn't feasible in Dave's case, so they agreed to live apart and visit when they could. "In all honesty," he writes, "it was a political marriage [her family] hoped would encourage me to somehow find a way to at least stop the ARVN attacks on the tribe."

~ ~ ~

As the Buon Eano project expanded, a second half-team of Americans came to help, led by Captain Ronald Shackleton of Detachment A-113. A Special Forces "A Team" consisted of two officers and ten noncoms (sergeants, specialists, or the occasional corporal or private first class). The CIA, however, often split the teams sent to Vietnam, as had happened to Arritola's detachment. Shackleton's executive officer, 1st Lieutenant Edward Bridges, and some enlisted men were sent elsewhere for a month or two. And at Buon Enao, each team was split further, so a few Americans could be salted among the "area development centers" that supported the project's expansion. Including Buon Enao, there would eventually be six of these centers, each with its own rapid-reaction Strike Force company of 120 men, a dispensary, and other amenities.

Recalling his experience at Buon Enao and later at Ban Don, Lieutenant Bridges echoed the American stereotype of the Highlanders. They were "excellent soldiers," he wrote. "Everybody worked as a team. I found them very brave under fire. . . . Yet, in another sense, Montagnards were like children. . . . Life to them was a series of stages, and death was nothing more than the means of moving from one stage to another." As he told the story, it was Shackleton's detachment that completed Buon Enao's defenses: "We built elephant traps, berms, punji stake pits, [and] burned or cut all the vegetation around the village. . . . By the time we finished it, the camp resembled forts built by the army during the Indian wars."

~ ~ ~

It is a given in warfare, as in physics, that any action brings an equal and opposite reaction. Dave Nuttle

28

remembers a "substantial" firefight about twice a week on average, meaning an engagement that lasted half an hour or more, with several hundred rounds fired at the enemy. One siege, at Buon Tang Ju in July, lasted three hours, and the defenders fired no fewer than 15,000 rounds. The Communists broke off before sunrise, as they always did, leaving two dead guerrillas behind, and blood trails showing that other casualties had been carried away. For their part, the villagers lost one man killed, along with his carbine; the widow was paid 2,000 piasters — $200 — in compensation.

The VC always attacked in the middle of the night, so they could get into position, try to overrun the defenses, and melt away, all in total darkness. They soon found that neighboring villages would send their own militia to help, and eventually that trucks would bring soldiers from farther off, so they learned to set an ambush on the trail or road that rescuers would have to take.

Philippe was one of those rescuers, driving a Ford or General Motors truck with a cab and an enclosed metal body that held a Strike Force platoon of twenty-four men. There were five of these cargo trucks at Buon Enao and each area development center, so that a company of 120 Strikers could be dispatched at a fairly high speed to any village that came under attack. In addition to the driver, two or three vehicle guards also rode along, to protect the truck on its way home.

This was the drill: When alerted by radio to a Viet

Cong attack, Cowboy drove at his best speed to the trailhead that gave access to the threatened village. As he neared the drop-off point, he slowed to a walking pace, so the Strikers could pile off the back. The other trucks followed the same drill, each dropping a platoon of Strikers — twenty-four men — at the trailhead. Then all five trucks returned as a convoy to their base, or they could pick up another company if needed.

Eventually the project added an open "Q truck" to be used when the Strike Force was venturing into hostile territory. In the back were six or eight men, protected by sandbags and armed with machineguns and grenade launchers. The name was adopted from the Royal Navy Q ships of the First World War, merchant vessels that would lure a German submarine into range, then suddenly deploy heavy guns to sink it.

From what I later saw of Cowboy, and from what others have told me about him, I suspect that he and his "Swedish K" took part in some of these firefights. Dave Nuttle argues otherwise: Philippe drove his cargo truck through to the designated trailhead, let the Strikers jump out, and then returned quietly to Buon Enao. Did he always follow this protocol? I find that very hard to believe.

The same was certainly true of the Green Berets who cycled through Buon Enao and the area development centers. In theory, the Americans were in Vietnam only as trainers and advisors, but nothing could have stopped them from joining combat, if only to set an example to the local troops, as in Gil Layton's recollection of the first patrol that encountered an actual Viet Cong, when a Green Beret had to fire the first shot.

In time, the Buon Enao project even got its own air force, courtesy of an "Air Commando" unit that was based at Bien Hoa near Saigon. The American pilots were pleased to have a steady supply of targets, and they assigned FACs — Forward Air Controllers — to work with the Green Berets on the ground. They kept several planes at the Ban Me Thuot airfield not far away, including a Douglas C-47 flare ship to illuminate a village under attack, and one or two North American T-28 training planes outfitted with two .50-caliber machineguns.

But the most useful aircraft, like Dave Nuttle himself, came from Kansas. This was a civilian lightplane adopted by the US Air Force as the U-10 Helio Courier. It could land and take off in such a short distance that two FACs, stationed at Buon Enao, chopped down a few trees east of the village and gave the camp its own Helio Courier airstrip. The Air Commandos also developed a technique for resupplying a besieged village from the air. Flying low and slow, they would drop a box of ammunition onto the thatch-and-bamboo roof of a longhouse, from which it tumbled to the ground without smashing either the box or the roof.

~ ~ ~

By the summer of 1962, the project had spread to two hundred villages with sixty thousand residents — Rhade, Jarai, and Mnong. Each had its own militia, backed up by a Strike Force company at Buon Enao or

31

an area development center. Really, nothing like it had ever happened in South Vietnam, nor would ever happen again.

The success didn't come without cost. Dave Nuttle estimates that forty villagers were killed over the course of that first year, including Strikers, militia, and civilians. But no American life was lost, and the same was apparently true of the LLDB team under Captain Khoai. The defenders were claiming a twelve-to-one kill ratio over the enemy, which if true meant upwards of four hundred VC dead.

Inevitably, Buon Enao became a regular stop for military and civilian VIPs. Dave remembers visits from General Victor ("Brute") Krulak of the US Marines; General Paul Harkins, then the senior US Army officer in Vietnam; and Major George Patton IV, son of the great tank commander of the Second World War. On the other hand, he recalls, Secretary of Defense Robert McNamara refused an invitation.

Of all the VIP tourists, the most significant was Ngo Dinh Nhu, who arrived with General Ton That Dinh, who commanded the ARVN divisions in the Highlands. The general was also a favorite of the ruling family. Stanley Karnow, in his admirable history of the Vietnam War, described Dinh as "a swaggering prima donna."

The villagers turned out in traditional costume. Boys and men danced around a tethered buffalo, beating gongs slung from their necks. A Rhade bullfighter first slashed the animal's hamstrings with a machete, then went into a dance, approaching the buffalo and backing off, feinting with a six-foot spear, until finally he drove it into the animal's side. While the animal died — it took a while — everyone drank from jugs of *numpai*, the evil tasting rice wine that was part of every Highlander ceremony. Then the guests were honored with a spoonful of brains from the slaughtered animal.

Also present was Lucien Conein, a veteran of both the French and American armies during the Second World War, and now an agent for the CIA. As Conein recalled the celebration some years later, General Dinh took Nhu aside and warned him that "the Americans have put an army at my back." Eighteen thousand Highlanders, he said, were already armed and trained — a considerable exaggeration for 1962, though it would come true in time.

The president's brother was stunned, as Conein told the story, and Nhu rejoined the festivities with his face "coldly impassive." From that day forward, he set out to bring the Village Defense program under Saigon's direct control, and thereby to destroy it. In this campaign, unfortunately, he had the help of the US Army.

Throughout history, countries have fielded elite units to perform tasks unsuited to the infantry. The United States was no exception, with Rogers Rangers during the French and Indian War (1754-1763), Quantrill's Raiders in the Civil War, and Merrill's Marauders in the Second World War. But the US Army was never comfortable with the notion, believing that the elites only took the best soldiers away from the infantry.

This mistrust was inherited by the Green Berets when Special Warfare branch was established in 1952. They soon began to affect the famous headgear, but by the spring of 1956, when I was sent to Fort Bragg as a propaganda writer for the Special Warfare Center, there wasn't a beret in sight. I was told that it had been forbidden by President Eisenhower himself, who as a four-star general had overseen the American and British conquest of Western Europe. Whether that was true or not, it is certain that John Kennedy, soon after he became Eisenhower's successor, made a point of approving the headgear, and soon berets of every color were gracing the heads of military units around the world.

But even the Kennedy administration had its skeptics about the Green Berets, notably General William Rosson, the Pentagon's go-to man for Special Warfare. Stationed in Saigon during the French debacle of 1954, Rosson was now an assistant to the Joint Chiefs of Staff. As such, he made the obligatory tour of Vietnam in April 1962, and Buon Enao of course was on the itinerary. Afterward, he filed a report to General Maxwell Taylor, the president's friend and soon-to-be Army Chief of Staff. The Green Berets assigned to the CIDG program were being used "improperly," Rosson said. He argued, and Taylor agreed, that instead of defending villages, they ought to be out in the puckerbrush, hunting and killing the Viet Cong.

The CIDG's sin, as the Army saw it, was that the program was being run by the spooks in the CIA. If the Green Berets were to function as soldiers, the Army needed to control them. The case was most eloquently stated by Lieutenant General Harold Johnson some years later: "Here was a mobile force supposed to be training guerrillas. . . . And what they did was build fortifications out of the Middle Ages. . . . Simply building little enclaves in each tribal area would not have very much utility as far as creating an environment for a free society was concerned."

Of course the generals had it exactly backward. As run by the CIA, Buon Enao was the very model of a *counterinsurgency* program, intended to show people that they would be better off siding with the government than with the Communists. The new plan was to send the Green Berets on the offensive, leading the Strikers in combat wherever they were needed. To the military, this was *unconventional warfare*, a wholly different approach, and one that has failed almost every time it has been tried.

So the US Army began to take control, in what it called Operation Switchback. Under the new thinking, the Strikers — recruited to serve in or near their home villages — would be grouped in battalions of 700 or 800 men and stationed wherever they were needed. In particular, the Army wanted to build a string of camps along the border with Cambodia and Laos, in hopes of halting the North Vietnamese infiltration that was supplying men and weapons to bolster the Viet Cong. Each camp would be run by a Vietnamese LLDB team, with the advice and help of a Special Forces A Team. So the US Army would control the

Green Berets, and Ngo Dinh Nhu would control the Strikers, making everyone in Saigon happy.

In September 1962, thirty-two of the Buon Enao villages were turned over to the Darlac province chief. To read the Special Forces histories, this step was proof of the project's resounding success. In fact, it was a sign that it would soon be dismantled.

Seeing the handwriting on the wall, Dave Nuttle did not renew his contract when his year with the CIA ended in October. "When I decided the Buon Enao project had been betrayed and destroyed," he wrote, "I elected to return to the U.S. And encouraged H'un to come with me as my wife. But H'un could not begin to think of leaving her family for any reason, so [we were] divorced under the usual procedures determined by Jarai tribal customs." By this time, they were the parents of a baby daughter, named Marina.

And that was the end of that — though not quite. Foolishly, as matters turned out, H'un decided to tie her future to that of Philippe Drouin. This too was a tribal marriage, though I'm told that her father, the Jarai chief Nay Moul, never recognized the match. If so, he was right: H'un had made a terrible mistake in marrying Philippe.

Portfolio:
Birth of the Strike Force

Buon Enao 1962: Rhade families lived together in a longhouse raised four feet above the ground on stilts, keeping the living quarters free of snakes and rodents and above the range of malarial mosquitoes. The "front step" was a notched log. The defended village of Buon Enao, with the forest closing in around it, was a far cry from the forts constructed for the Civilian Irregular Defense Groups after they were militarized in 1963. (US government)

Sergeant Paul Campbell, a Special Forces medic, carried no weapon and wore civilian clothes when he toured Rhade villages and held a sick call. Here he examines a child held by its father. The sergeant and David Nuttle scouted out a likely place to begin the Village Defenders project in October 1961, visiting two dozen Rhade villages around the provincial capital of Ban Me Thuot. (US government)

Y Ju, the Buon Enao headman, talks things over with Dave Nuttle, who headed up the project that spread across much of Darlac province. Y Ju's weapon is a modified M-1 carbine with a folding stock. More than a thousand carbines were distributed to the CIDG in the first half of 1962, along with bolt-action rifles, pistols, and sub-machineguns. (David Nuttle)

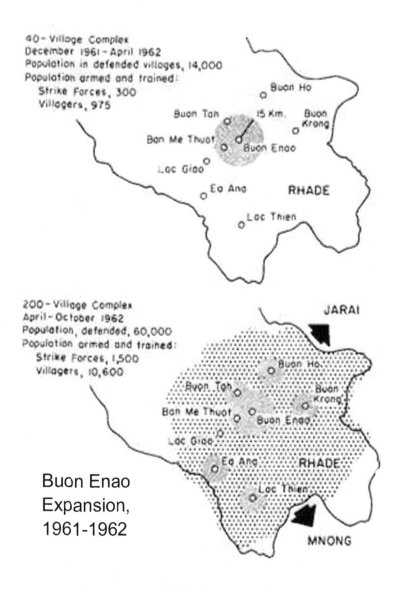

40 - Village Complex
December 1961 - April 1962
Population in defended villages, 14,000
Population armed and trained:
  Strike Forces, 300
  Villagers, 975

Buon Ho
Buon Ton   15 Km   Buon Krong
Ban Me Thuot   Buon Enao
Loc Giao
Eo Ang   RHADE
Loc Thien

200 - Village Complex
April - October 1962
Population, defended, 60,000
Population armed and trained:
  Strike Forces, 1,500
  Villagers, 10,600

JARAI

Buon Ho
Buon Ton   Buon Krong
Ban Me Thuot   Buon Enao
Loc Giao
Eo Ang   RHADE
Loc Thien

MNONG

Buon Enao
Expansion,
1961-1962

*Buon Enao was a model of counterinsurgency. Two
hundred villages joined the project, defended by
10,400 armed militiamen and 1,500 "Strikers" of the
Civilian Irregular Defense Group. (US government)*

To me, the Highlanders seemed more Polynesian than Asian, and that was certainly true of H'un with her long, curly hair and tawny skin. She would have been 18 in this photo, posing with a Highland flower (not an orchid, though it looks like one) and wearing traditional Jarai costume. Married in turn to Dave Nuttle and Philippe Drouin, she lived in her parents' longhouse in the village of R'bol and worked as an interpreter for the USAID mission in Cheo Reo. (David Nuttle)

41

How Philippe Became the Cowboy

I T WASN'T LONG before Buon Enao had to pay the price of going on the offensive. No fewer than three A Teams joined the project in August 1962: Detachment A-334, led by Captain Terry Cordell; A-214, led by Captain Eugene Abernathy, and A-223, led by 1st Lieutenant James McFadden.

Cordell and his men were centered at Buon Enao itself, replacing Ronald Shackleton's team. Lieutenant McFadden, having flown from Okinawa in "an unmarked C-47, with a Taiwanese pilot," was given an old jeep, a US Army two-and-a-half-ton truck, and a squad of Rhade Strikers, and sent to build a new camp at the village of Buon Tha. The third team is something of a mystery, but Captain Abernathy and his men were probably divided among the area development centers.

Sergeant Arthur Fields has left us the best account of Green Berets in combat during the Buon Enao years. In a very few weeks, he and the rest of Lieutenant McFadden's team fortified Buon Tha, built a dispensary, and trained the village militia. They also pushed toward Ban Don, fifty kilometers northwest of Ban Me Thuot and closer to Cambodia. "As we advanced toward the Cambodian border," Fields writes, "the VC started emptying out the villages that we had not yet reached — taking the villagers into the jungle and going underground. We discovered the VC had established a training camp in the foothills of the Cu Ken mountains near Ban Don along the Song Srepok river. This VC base stood between us and Ban Don, so we decided to take it out."

Captain Cordell at Buon Enao functioned rather like a "B Team" commander, to whom the other teams were responsible — yet he was as new to the country as they were. And Dave Nuttle, who might have been a restraining influence, was gone from Vietnam. Left unchecked, the Green Berets and the Air Commandos cooked up what may have been the first heliborne combat operation of the Vietnam War, on October 15-16, 1962.

Three Piasecki H-21 "Flying Banana" helicopters carried the assault force to the drop zone south of Ban Don. The Strikers promptly captured two guerrillas, and there were signs that many more were in the area, so Art Fields called on a twin-engine Douglas B-26 attack plane to bomb and strafe the area. Two T-28 Nomad armed trainers, each with two .50-caliber machineguns, also provided air support, terrifying the Strikers who had seen warplanes only as a threat to their own villages. Captain Cordell scouted the area in the U-10 Helio Courier with an Air Force pilot and crewman, coordinating ground operations and spotting targets for the warplanes.

The Viet Cong naturally targeted the plane flying low and slow. The Helio Courier was hit, burst into flame, and dove into the ground, killing all three men aboard. The Green Berets and the Strikers formed a perimeter around the crash site and held it through the night. In the morning, a Sikorsky H-34 came down from Pleiku to retrieve the bodies under fire; when an Air Commando T-28 swooped into suppress the Viet Cong, it too was shot down, the pilot badly injured but alive.

Later, Art Fields and his men surrounded the VC anti-aircraft squad and captured the weapon that had brought down two warplanes and killed three Americans. It was a Browning Automatic Rifle, first issued to American troops in 1917, as the United States entered the First World War.

Before another year was over, the Green Berets were withdrawn from Buon Enao, and counter-insurgency was abandoned in favor of killing the Viet Cong wherever they could be found. Viewed from the perspective of fifty-odd years, our strategy in Vietnam makes no sense whatever. We used our troops like checkers on a board, jumping from place to place at the whim of commanders who themselves never stayed in one place very long.

~ ~ ~

Philippe Drouin, meanwhile, left Buon Enao and moved to Cheo Reo to be near his wife and step-daughter. H'un's village was probably the settlement of R'bol, north of the town center.

Cheo Reo today is called Ayun Pa and has a population of thirty-five thousand, spread over 250 square kilometers. I remember it as a single honky-tonk street lined with ramshackle shops, where a Chinese merchant sold me Coca Cola in a glass, with a chunk of ice and who knows what sorts of wildlife. There was also an Esso station, headquarters for the province chief, the USAID mission where H'un worked, and, I was told, no fewer than seven brothels. It wasn't nearly as large or sophisticated as Ban Me Thuot, but it had all the essentials.

Southwest of Cheo Reo, the airfield was surfaced with linked sheets of steel with holes in it — pierced-steel planking, which the US military called PSP. And a kilometer or so northwest was a Special Forces camp known as Buon Beng. Like Buon Enao, it was basically just a fenced village, with an all-Jarai Strike Force protecting it. As I wrote in my journal in June 1964:

"The camp and the village are one and the same. Longhouses alternate with the Special Forces buildings, and pigs wallow in the zigzag trench that runs around the perimeter. Dark-skinned troopers saluted us, and dark-skinned children goggled at us. The troopers wear green fatigues; the children are naked."

(A "fatigue," in the mid-century US Army, was a work detail, and "fatigues" denoted the olive-green cotton worn on such an assignment and also in warm-weather combat. Today the more elevated term is "battledress," but I can't bring myself to use it.)

You'll notice that I made no mention of the Vietnamese LLDB troops who supposedly ran the camp. That's because they kept a low profile, letting the Americans manage things however they wanted. Indeed, I once saw a Green Beret grab his "counterpart" by the shirt-front and shake him like a naughty boy.

The camp was established in August 1962, by Detachment A-213 under 1st Lieutenant Marshall Stogner. They were replaced in January 1963 by Captain Wesley Herrlein and Detachment A-412. One of those two officers hired Philippe and dubbed him "the Cowboy," which was a fairly common nickname for any indigenous soldier who affected a tough-guy swagger. This was probably fairly early in the history of Buon Beng, since H'un and Marina were living nearby, in the longhouse of Nay Moul.

As Cowboy told the story, he was the indigenous commander of the Strike Force battalion until fired by "Captain Wesley." This was almost certainly a fantasy. Even if Wesley Herrlein was one of those Green Berets who ignored his LLDB counterpart, I doubt he could have fired the battalion commander. An interpreter, on the other hand, was a personal aide, and hiring and firing him would certainly have been the captain's privilege. In any event, "the Cowboy" eventually found another berth at Duc Co, 160 kilometers northwest and just 12 kilometers from Cambodia. It was one of seven camps being established along the border in hopes of blocking troops and supplies coming down the Ho Chi Minh Trail from North Vietnam.

Arguably, Duc Co was the most important of the seven. It perched by the side of Highway 19, along which any North Vietnamese army must travel to reach the South China Sea and thereby cut South Vietnam in half. This was more than just paranoia on the part of the Saigon government and the US military: it was indeed how Ho Chi Minh and his military genius, Vo Nguyen Giap, intended to conquer South Vietnam.

Unlike the defended villages of Buon Enao and Buon Beng, Duc Co was built for the purpose – a perfect square, set in the open and containing an internal square as a redoubt in case the VC got through. The outer wall was guarded by Claymore mines, coils of razor wire, and the usual punji sticks. The Strikers, the LLDB, and the Green Berets slept in sandbagged bunkers, though some Highlanders had brought their families with them, to live in the traditional elevated huts. The camp was built in the summer of 1963 by Detachment A-736 under Captain Edwin Griffith, who brought Cowboy with him.

By this time, the Special Forces had built out their Vietnam presence to thirty-six A Teams in as many CIDG camps, many of them in the Highlands. They were supervised by four regional B Teams, one in each military district of South Vietnam, with the whole effort commanded by a C Team in Nha Trang on the coast.

Toward the end of August 1963, a big Boeing CH-47 Chinook helicopter brought Captain Johnnie Corns and the men of Detachment A-752 to the dusty, red-clay airstrip across the road from Duc Co. Corns was disappointed by the briefing he'd received in Pleiku, and even more disappointed when he saw the camp Captain Griffith was turning over to him. He judged it to be poorly located and its defenses badly laid out. He later relocated the machineguns to his own satis-faction, and cleared the brush obscuring their field of fire, but the B Team in Pleiku refused his request to move the camp to a more commanding position.

Cowboy, though, was a pleasant surprise. When Corns and his team first came through the gate, the interpreter was standing negligently by one of the huts, roofed with tin and walled with bamboo mats. "I thought someone was playing a joke on us," Corns wrote many years later. "He could have been the Asian version of the Marlboro Man. Cowboy boots, jeans, complete with a large bronco-riding emblem on a western belt buckle, and a . . . long sleeve shirt with various white stripes crisscrossing over a sky blue background. Atop his head was a smart, western style hat and over his eyes was a pair of large aviator style sunglasses. Sergeant [George] Manuel looked a little bit sheepish as he said, 'Sir, that is Cowboy. He's your personal interpreter.'"

"He's very good, Captain Corns," the outgoing commander assured him. "A little bit flashy, but a damn good interpreter."

Indeed, Corns came to like, admire, and trust Cowboy, who not only enabled him to communicate with the Strikers, the Vietnamese province chief, and the LLDB commander, but also appointed himself as the American's personal bodyguard. Cowboy, Corns decided, was the most natural soldier at Duc Co.

This judgment was cemented during a patrol to the border that ran into a VC ambush. Cowboy was the man who instantly reacted, grabbing the platoon's BAR from the Striker who was carrying it. The Browning Automatic Rifle weighed nineteen pounds, double the weight of a standard infantry rifle and triple that of the M-1 carbine then favored by American advisors in Vietnam. Yet Cowboy easily fired it from the hip, like a Hollywood hero, blasting the forest where the guerrillas were concealed. That silenced the ambush.

Later on that same mission, Cowboy borrowed the captain's Leica camera (given to him by the CIA paymaster who each month flew into Duc Co with a bag of piasters to pay the Strikers, and who had requested this clandestine patrol) into Cambodia to photograph a new airstrip. Reading Corns's account, it's hard to escape the conclusion that, at least on this occasion, Cowboy was the leader who assessed the situation, decided the best course of action, and took a few picked men across the border, where the Strikers and the Americans were forbidden to go.

"He was almost too good to be true," Corns concluded. "But to a man, I and every other member of my team decided that he was that good. . . . There was no one else I would prefer to have at my back and at my side. I guessed he was the bravest among us. . . ."

On a lighter note, the captain enjoyed Cowboy's use of American idiom, no doubt gained from Hollywood Westerns. "That'll be the day," he would say, quoting John Wayne from *The Searchers*. Or "Sorry don't get it done, Dude," from *Rio Bravo*. Or "Out here a man settles his own problems," from *The Man Who Shot Liberty Valance*.

A Front to Liberate the Oppressed

BY THE SUMMER of 1963, the Civilian Irregular Defense Groups had grown to 18,000 Strikers nationwide, most of them recruited from ethnic or religious minorities. In the Highlands, that generally meant the aboriginal tribes. So General Ton That Dinh's nightmare had come true, though the army at his back was country-wide and without a common agenda. The general, meanwhile, had moved to Saigon, where he was put in command of the military district surrounding the capital. A favorite of the ruling family, Dinh was soon deep in the plots and counter-plots that roiled the city that fall.

The Americans, from John Kennedy on down to the diplomats, generals, and spies in Saigon, were weary of Ngo Dinh Diem, who seemed less interested in winning the war than in punishing his internal enemies. Buddhism was his most recent target — the religion of most Vietnamese, though not of the Ngo family and its French-educated supporters.

On June 11, 1963, a monk named Quang Duc responded to the regime's oppression by seating himself on a pillow in the middle of a street intersection, a few blocks from the presidential palace. A colleague soaked him with gasoline from a five-gallon plastic jerry can. Quang Duc lit a match, immolating himself as hundreds watched, prayed, and took photographs that next day were on the front pages of newspapers around the world. "No news picture in history has generated so much emotion," said President Kennedy — a Catholic like Diem, though with an infinitely better instinct for governing.

Kennedy's first step toward ridding himself of the Ngo family was to recall Frederick Nolting, whose policy toward the Saigon government was to "take it slow and easy." The new ambassador would be Henry Cabot Lodge Jr., whose virtues included the fact that he was a Republican. (Kennedy had become a US Senator by winning Lodge's seat in 1952, and he'd gone on to win the presidency by defeating the Nixon-Lodge ticket in 1960.) Bipartisanship was expected of American governments in those years. Besides, having a Republican running things in Saigon would give Kennedy cover if things went bad, as indeed they would.

There were other differences between then and now: Ambassadors had more power, and events moved more slowly. It was August 26 before Lodge sat down for a stilted and discouraging meeting with President Diem. Four more monks had "barbecued" themselves by this time, in Madame Nhu's contemptuous term, and LLDB troops (disguised as ARVN) had sacked Buddhist pagodas, arrested hundreds of monks and nuns, and killed scores of people in Saigon, Hue, and other cities. Even Madame Nhu's father, South Vietnam's ambassador to the United States, resigned in protest.

Within three days of his arrival, Lodge decided

that the Ngo family had to go, and soon enough the Kennedy administration swung behind him. Or perhaps it was a setup, and Lodge was sent to Saigon for the express purpose of getting rid of Diem, Nhu, and Madame Nhu with her clueless sound bites. However it happened, JFK was about to cross the Rubicon, taking the step that in time would lead to 58,000 American dead, the ruination of a small country, a virtual civil war at home and, in the end, humiliation for the United States and victory for Hanoi.

It began with a double set of murders. The first to be killed was Colonel Le Quang Tung, the head of the hated LLDB, on the night of November 1, 1963. Tung's brother died with him. The next morning, the plotters captured President Diem and *his* brother, imprisoned them in the hull of an armored personnel carrier, and shot and stabbed them to death. General Duong Van Minh became head of a military junta, with a figurehead civilian president to please the Americans. "Big Minh," as the general was popularly known, would spend much of the following year in a revolving door with General Nguyen Khanh, as they took turns overthrowing one another.

John Kennedy did not long survive the Ngo brothers. On November 23, JFK was murdered in his turn, and everything slid downhill from there. Perhaps those deaths did not change history, but they certainly ended any chance that Diem or Kennedy might have changed the course of the war. It would last twelve more years, spilling over into North Vietnam, Cambodia, Laos, and even Thailand, and as many as three million people would die before their time.

~ ~ ~

Cowboy, too, was moving on. Perhaps he wanted to be closer to H'un and Marina, who had visited him only twice at Duc Co. Perhaps FULRO had advanced its plans for rebellion, with Buon Beng as a suitable place for him. (At this point, FULRO was mostly a Rhade enterprise. Married to a Jarai woman, familiar with the Buon Beng Strike Force, and able to get along with Americans, Cowboy would have been the perfect emissary.) Or perhaps he had simply been too open in his contempt for Captain Minh, the LLDB commander at Duc Co.

In December 1963, when Cowboy was absent on business of his own, Captain Minh requested a private interview with Captain Corns — i.e., without waiting for the interpreter's return. Corns agreed, since his counterpart spoke English well enough for most purposes. With the utmost delicacy, Minh set out to undermine the interpreter, whom he accused of manifold offenses.

First, he accused Cowboy of regularly taking a government truck for his personal errands — indeed, had even now driven it to another Special Forces camp for some dubious purpose. Second, he had "made some trouble with high-level officials in Saigon." Finally, there was this letter, which Minh displayed for the American's benefit. It recommended "Mister Philip Drouin" for employment as "a superior interpreter-translator with a thorough knowledge of

53

tactics," and it was an obvious forgery. The signature block read "Johnnie A. Corn, Captain, Armor," though the captain's middle initial was *h*, his surname ended in an *s*, and his Army branch was infantry, not armor.

Corns made no comment on the letter, which he guessed had been written by Cowboy with the help of the team sergeant, George Manuel. "I simply had chosen sides between Philippe and Minh," he explained in his memoir of his time in Vietnam. "I viewed Philippe as the finest soldier in the Duc Co camp, I viewed Minh as a little bureaucrat, caught up in the urgency to keep his bosses in Saigon content [so he could] keep his job and ensure his future."

Some of Minh's accusations were true, and perhaps they all were. On December 17, Cowboy turned up at Buon Beng and presented his oddly phrased forgery to Captain Crews McCulloch, commander of the newly arrived Detachment A-424. As McCulloch tells the story:

"Philippe Drouin arrived at camp Buon Beng with his wife and small daughter in an old dilapidated three-quarter-ton Army truck and a letter of recommendation from another camp. I immediately hired him. . . . He quickly proved himself to be even better than our chief interpreter, Kpa Doh. He was fluent in English, French, Vietnamese, and about five tribal dialects. He hated the Vietnamese and did not like to speak their language. He soon became like a shadow to me. If I went on patrol he insisted that he must go. He was a good fighter under fire, and would stay fast until the last round was fired."

Captain McCulloch became so fond of Cowboy that he loaned him the .357 magnum revolver he'd brought to Vietnam as his personal weapon, along with its leather holster and belt with cartridge loops. "From then until I left Vietnam," McCulloch says, "he wore it constantly with the belt sloped and the holster tied to his leg with a rawhide strap." The transition to Cowboy was complete.

The team's second-in-command was likewise impressed. Jim Morris was still a first lieutenant when he set out for the war, but had received his captain's bars en route. Like many Americans of the time – including me! – he was enchanted by Vietnam, the Highlands, Cheo Reo, the Buon Beng Strike Force, the Highlanders . . . and Cowboy. Morris was working on the camp accounts, an awful job and one that therefore usually fell to the executive officer, when he became aware that someone was standing over him. As he recounted the meeting in *War Story*, his wonderful memoir of his time in Vietnam:

"When I looked up, there was a three-fifth scale model of a Choctaw Indian standing there. That's what he looked like with that brown skin and those high cheekbones. An infectious grin spread all over his little Montagnard face. Size five Cowboy boots. Sears, Roebuck jeans and a jean jacket over an immaculate white shirt. He stood with all his weight on one hip. One hand was in his hip pocket and with the other he dragged a Salem cigarette. He was two months overdue for a haircut and both his eyes were cupped by wraparound shades. Goddamnedest thing I ever saw, a Montagnard drugstore Cowboy."

They negotiated a salary of 6500 piasters a month — about $650 today, and triple what an honest bureaucrat could earn in Saigon. Cowboy then asked for another 1400 piasters in "jump pay," since he'd qualified as a "para" in the French Colonial Army. "Cowboy," Morris said. "You have found the way to touch my heart. Paratrooping is my religion. What's yours?"

"VC," the interpreter said. "My religion is to kill VC."

~ ~ ~

The possibility that Cowboy moved to Buon Beng on instructions from FULRO is supported by other developments that winter. In February 1964, General Khanh in Saigon ordered the release of Y Bham Enoul and the other nationalists who'd been imprisoned since 1958, first at Nha Trang, then in the old imperial capital of Hue. To further placate the Highlanders, Y Bham was given the newly created post of deputy to the Darlac province chief in Ban Me Thuot, and Paul Nur got the same post in Kontum to the north. These concessions persuaded them not to throw in their lot with the militants at Camp le Rolland, for the time being anyhow. They were bound to be disappointed: the province chiefs were not only ethnic Vietnamese, but officers in the ARVN, and it's not likely they paid much attention to their new deputies.

With or without the knowledge of Y Bham Enoul and Paul Nur, and with the nudging of Norodom Sihanouk in Phnom Penh, FULRO was advancing its plans for a Highlander rebellion. Cowboy and Kpa Doh seem to have joined the plot very early. And Nay Luett — Rcom H'un's brother-in-law, hence Cowboy's in-law as well — had hired on as a truck driver at the Buon Beng camp, near Cheo Reo, soon after he was freed from prison. Given his age, his language ability, and his imposing bearing, Nay Luett was grossly over-qualified for driving a truck; almost certainly he had a larger plan in mind.

~ ~ ~

On their first night ambush, Jim Morris and Cowboy each carried an AR-15, the lightweight, 5.56 mm (.223 caliber) assault rifle designed by Eugene Stoner and licensed to the Colt's Manufacturing Company. Though the US Army turned down an early version, Colt sold a few thousand to the Malaysian army, the US Air Force, and some American police forces, and in 1964 Special Forces began to test the rifle in Vietnam. It would evolve into one of the most famous and most popular weapons ever built, rivaled only by the much heavier Kalashnikov AK-47.

The patrol also had a machinegun, two BARs, and a carbine for each man not otherwise armed. At Fort Bragg a few years earlier, I'd been issued a carbine with the serial number 1048802 — a number I'll never forget, because the weapon gave me so much and such frequent trouble. Whenever I used it on the firing range, it jammed so thoroughly that I had to bring it back to the company armorer for repair. Still, the carbine was just the right size and weight for the diminutive Vietnamese, and American advisors with

ARVN battalions invariably carried it, so perhaps 1048802 was an outlier. In any event, the ambush party had thirteen weapons that could fire at full automatic, giving it the firepower of a full company of Second World War GIs. When the Viet Cong marched through the ambush site, they left six bodies on the trail.

"I moved from one dark shape to another," Morris recalled, "making sure they were dead. . . .

"When we came to the last one I moved in on him and he raised up his arms extended, eyes wide. . . . I said, 'Good, we got a pris. . . .'

"Cowboy stitched him up the middle with his AR-15. He didn't even twitch."

"Goddamn it," Morris said, "we could have got some good information from that guy."

"Sorry," said Cowboy. "I get, you know, excited."

"He was really something," as Morris concluded the story. ". . . and it was a measure of my attitude at the time that I loved him like a brother."

~ ~ ~

Crews McCulloch also had an ambush story, though in this case it was the Strikers who were caught short. And they were far from home, near the Chu Pong massif, eighty kilometers northwest of Buon Beng and not far from Cowboy's former haunt at Duc Co. This area would later become famous as the Ia Drang Valley, where a US Army cavalry battalion was savaged by a regiment of North Vietnamese. (The North Vietnamese actually fared worse, though that's usually ignored in histories of the war.) Running out of water, the Buon Beng Strikers followed a compass line to the nearest stream, which may have been the Ia Drang itself. They broke discipline and splashed into the water.

No sooner did McCulloch regain control and start moving his men along the riverbank than they came under fire. The captain's boot-heel was clipped by a bullet and both his sergeants were badly wounded, as were several Strikers. However, there were about a hundred of them, and they managed to rush the VC, scatter them, and in a bit of luck contact a passing helicopter that evacuated the worst cases.

"Cowboy was visibly shaken," McCulloch recalled. "He told me later that he had never been that scared and felt certain that he would be killed." His tongue loosened by the adrenalin boost of combat, the interpreter went on to tell the captain an astonishing story — about the *Front Unifié de Lutte des Races Opprimées*, about his role in it, and about the uprising they were planning.

Back at Buon Beng three days later, McCulloch requested the B Team commander, Major Richard Buck in Pleiku, to come down to the camp, meet the conspirators, and hear their story. The conference included Cowboy of course, along with Kpa Doh, Nay Luett, and Ksor Kok, one of the young Jarai militants who'd followed Y Dhon Adrong to Camp le Rolland. Among other things, Jim Morris recalled, the Americans learned that Kpa Doh had stashed some 20,000 piasters of FULRO money in the A Team safe — about

$2,000 today — to support the rebellion.

Incredibly, this bit of intelligence was not only ignored but loudly resented. McCulloch and Morris told me similar though not identical stories of how they were bullied by American intelligence operatives – whether US Army or CIA isn't clear – who accused them of spreading false stories of a Highlander uprising. Perhaps somebody in Saigon took the warning seriously, but if so, preparations to counter the rebellion were poor or nonexistent.

~ ~ ~

It may have been on this occasion that Jim Morris had a chat with Major Buck about the location of Buon Beng. The major didn't like the camp — didn't like the pig shit, in Morris's opinion, nor the other annoyances that came with setting up a military operation in an aboriginal village. He wanted it moved to a new location. Morris, on the contrary, enjoyed the bustle and confusion of Buon Beng, even at the expense of occasionally stepping in a mess.

He also believed the location gave the Strike Force a tactical edge. "We could leave just before dawn, in trucks," as he explained in *War Story,* "and [the VC] might know when we left, and they might know which direction we were going, but they couldn't watch the whole road to see where we dismounted, so we could get into their areas undetected. We got to romp and stomp a bit because of that."

Morris made this argument to the B Team commander. "But it doesn't fit the concept," Major Buck replied. And that was the end of that. In the US Army, the concept rules. And when an officer disagrees with a superior, he just salutes and gets on with the job: a captain doesn't argue with a major.

Romping and Stomping
from Buon Beng

SURE ENOUGH, when I turned up in Pleiku in June 1964 with my camera, Boy Scout knapsack, and black-market C rations, Major Buck dashed my hopes of visiting a camp along the Cambodian border. "Every reporter wants to write about the Ho Chi Minh Trail," he said, but I — I would have the privilege of writing about Buon Beng.

"You'll get to see the old and the new," he promised. The camp should have been closed down long since, but the province chief was afraid to let the Americans leave the area, so they'd struck a compromise. Buon Beng would stay open for the time being, but the main effort would shift to a Forward Operating Base in "Indian Country," as the Americans called the area where the Viet Cong could operate with impunity. That, I had learned, was just about everything outside the larger towns and major roads — and the roads, too, as soon as the sun went down.

"And where is the FOB?" I asked, wondering what I was getting into.

He spread blunt fingers over the map of II Corps, in a gesture that covered perhaps fifty square kilometers. "Somewhere along there," he said. "I don't have the coordinates because we're having a little trouble with communications. The call sign at Buon

Beng is 'Barry,' and mine is 'Six Eight Baseball Glove.' That's all you need to know."

I thanked him, went outside, and sat down in the shade while I wrote up the interview. Six Eight Baseball Glove, as I described him, was "a short, chunky major with a splendid scar, curving along his left cheek from the corner of his eye to the corner of his mouth. The scar makes his mouth droop when he smiles, and gives his voice a slurred quality when he speaks. I was disappointed when a clerk-typist told me that it resulted from an automobile accident, not hand-to-hand combat at Guadalcanal or the Chosin Reservoir."

When I was home that fall and drafting the novel that became *Incident at Muc Wa*, I'm afraid I turned the major into something of a buffoon. An internet search now tells me that, between Korea and Vietnam, Rick Buck managed to accumulate *two* Silver Stars, *seven* Bronze Stars, *eight* Purple Hearts, and the Combat Infantryman's Badge, which is very impressive, especially the eight medals for combat wounds. (The scriptwriter for the movie, *Go Tell the Spartans*, treated him more kindly, in a role filled by the great Burt Lancaster.) But in 1964 I regarded Major Buck as a figure of fun.

This was Camp Holloway on the outskirts of Pleiku, a wonderful town where I could cool myself for the first time since landing at Saigon a month earlier. At 2,500 feet above sea level, Pleiku that afternoon was 90 degrees Fahrenheit in the sun and a delightful 70 degrees in the shade. The B Team headquarters was a low-roofed wooden building with three flags flying in front of it: the Stars and Stripes, the yellow-and-red banner of South Vietnam, and the silhouette of a big-antlered stag. The clerk-typist who told me about the scar also explained that the stag was the major's personal emblem. It flew whenever he was in residence, like the royal standard at Windsor Castle.

The clerk-typist's briefing also included the information that there were forty-one Special Forces officers and men in the Pleiku B Team, overseeing eighteen A Teams scattered through the Highlands, with two officers and ten noncoms in each. I did the math and concluded that there were 257 Green Berets in II Corps, and maybe a thousand altogether in South Vietnam. That was a considerable portion — five percent! — of all the American soldiers in the country.

~ ~ ~

A little trouble with communications! That should have warned me. But with the optimism of the young, I packed my gear, hitched a ride to the airfield, and climbed aboard the De Havilland Otter that a transportation clerk told me would stop at Buon Beng. The Otter was a beefy, single-engine plane, made in Canada and designed to operate out of short, rough runways. In Vietnam, the US Army became the world's largest operator of these redoubtable bush planes, designated the U-1A.

Alas, the pilots weren't expecting me, nor had they ever heard of Buon Beng. I explained that when we were over a town named Cheo Reo, they should call for "Barry," whereupon somebody would come out to the airstrip and pick me up. They checked their code book and said, yes, there was a Special Forces camp near Cheo Reo, but its call sign was "Blaze." However, I was welcome to ride along, so I sat on a pile of parachutes for the one-hour flight over the mountains to Cheo Reo. In all my flights around Vietnam, in helicopters, light planes, and cargo craft, I was only once asked if I had "orders" authorizing my presence, and in that case I simply said yes, I did, and the pilot didn't ask to see them.

The Otter was making the rounds of Special Forces camps so the Americans could "jump for payday," it being a requirement that every Green Beret keep current as a parachutist. We landed on Cheo Reo's pierced-steel runway at two o'clock. A jeep ambulance was waiting for us, sweat running from the faces of three men perched on its hood. We were halfway to the sea from Pleiku, and only 545 feet above sea level, so the temperature was correspondingly higher. I too was sweating by the time I'd walked over and introduced myself. Yes, they were from Buon Beng. No, they weren't here to meet me.

Two of them adjusted their berets and went off to make their payday jumps, leaving me in the charge of Sergeant Edwin Kuligowski – called Ski, of course. He had the most prominent face I'd ever seen: jaw, ears, nose. Even his eyes were prominent. His team was based at Bishigawa, on Okinawa, the Japanese island largely covered by American military bases. Captain McCulloch and the rest of team A-424 had returned to the US in May, to be replaced by Captain Charles

Judge and A-433. It was an insane system, six months here and six months there. (In time, Special Forces would extend the Vietnam tours to a year, which was much better, but still far from ideal.)

The ambulance was to accommodate any jumper who experienced "a disabling PLF," with the acronym standing for Parachute Landing Fall. At Fort Bragg in 1956, the 1st Radio Broadcast and Leaflet Battalion — that's what we were called! — had been tasked with developing a safety poster for the 82nd Airborne Division. My caption, lettered upon a painting of a plaster walking cast, was *Don't Make a Disabling PLF*. For this, the US Army had paid me $80 a month.

After the Otter was airborne with the two Green Berets, Sergeant Ski handed me his rifle and went over to mark the landing zone with a smoke grenade. I would soon learn that the ruling instinct of every Special Forces soldier was to put a weapon in the hands of any civilian in sight.

There was a breeze aloft, so the pilot allowed for wind drift, only to have the breeze fade just as the parachutes blossomed. As a result, both men went into the woods. Sergeant Ski and I climbed into the ambulance and went out to rescue them. We found the first man in a sort of corral, surrounded by a fence made from woven thorn branches, and filled with waist-high tree stumps. He trudged out, carrying his parachute and sweating. After the sergeant had ribbed him sufficiently, I learned that this was the team commander, Captain Charles Judge. He was as short as Major Buck in Pleiku, though younger and leaner.

He had a widow's peak coming down the center of his square forehead.

We found the other jumper after some searching. Sergeant Charles Coffing — called Coffee —was one of Buon Beng's radio operators. He was mild and youthful, a world away from the stereotype of the Green Berets.

After returning the parachutes to the Otter, which had landed while we were beating around in the bush, we drove for a few kilometers over a dirt road to Buon Beng. An elderly Highlander weaved across the compound, saluting every light-skinned face he encountered, including mine. "That's our cook," one of the Americans said. "There'll be good chow tonight — he's been to a numpai party in town."

Numpai parties, I learned, were the bane of Special Forces teams in the Highlands. Whenever a man did something notable, the jug was brought out and a buffalo or pig roasted over a fire, charring the outside but barely warming the inside. The rice wine had fermented beneath a layer of leaves, to prevent the precious gasses from escaping. The guest of honor was expected to squat in front of the jug and drink from a long bamboo tube. When he had drunk his fill, the host would pour water onto the leaves, to see how much had been consumed. A canteen cup full, about a pint, was considered a fair round, and five or six rounds a fair proof of manhood.

Few American stomachs could withstand the combination of murky wine and bloody meat. I never did have a chance to taste numpai, but one Green

Beret recalled that the more he drank of it, the worse it seemed, until "it finally tasted like a combination of sugar, water and vomit."

~ ~ ~

There were five Strike Force companies at Buon Beng, about eight hundred men altogether, recruited from the Jarai villages in and around Cheo Reo. In theory, an LLDB team — Vietnamese Special Forces — ran the operation, with the Americans as their advisors. But nobody at Buon Beng seemed to take them seriously. The Highlanders hated them, the Americans barely tolerated them, and even the Vietnamese seemed to agree that their job was just to make the system look good on paper. The camp commander lived in town, and turned up only when he was needed to greet a visiting dignitary. I didn't qualify for a greeting, if only because nobody had known I was coming.

The Jarai were sturdy, dark, and coarse-featured, like the Highlanders I'd seen in Pleiku. There was one exception, who impressed me so much that I devoted several paragraphs to him in my journal:

"The only handsome man in the group is the interpreter, whose name is Philippe Drouin but whom the Americans call Cowboy. He cuts a dashing figure in an expensive, broad brimmed camouflage hat and tiger striped camouflage fatigues. He carries a hunting knife strapped to his waist. He earned his nickname from his habit of demonstrating his fast draw with this knife, using Viet Cong prisoners as his audience and target. Supposedly he has killed twenty-two men with that knife, smiling his brilliant smile. . . .

"As the man who is the voice of the Americans in Buon Beng, Cowboy enjoys a tremendous importance, and he shows it in every line of his well-tailored body. None of the Americans speak much Jarai, and none of the Montagnards except Cowboy and one other interpreter — called Little Cowboy— speak much English."

About that smile: It was indeed brilliant. Cowboy had large teeth, and I think a bit of an overbite, so they were immediately and almost dazzlingly visible when he smiled. He was twenty-eight that summer. He had been at Buon Beng for about six months, which was five months longer than Captain Judge and his team, and supposedly he'd served here once before.

Thanks to Cowboy's ingratiating manner, his Cheo Reo connections, and his warrior instincts, he had made himself into the most important man in the camp, much as he had done at Duc Co. As for the interpreter known as Little Cowboy, I'm guessing that he was Kpa Doh. Other teams had other nicknames for him, including Pardo and Bardo.

Unlike Jim Morris of A-424, the new team had drunk the Kool Aid that Major Buck had brewed at Camp Holloway. Captain Judge told me that their primary duty was to close down Buon Beng and build a new camp at the Forward Operating Base. "We're supposed to be on the frontier," he drawled in a very good imitation of John Wayne, "and this don't hardly qualify any more." (Had he picked up that tic from Cowboy?)

He led me on a tour of the camp, which did indeed

have a settled look. The buildings used by the Americans — mess hall, battalion headquarters, supply room, sleeping quarters — were set on concrete slabs. There were permanent mortar positions inside the barbed wire, with a poncho draped over the weapon to keep it dry, giving it a scarecrow look. The Highlanders' longhouses were set high on stilts and oriented north-south, in the native fashion. They'd been intended as barracks for the men, with their wives and children living outside the barbed wire, but as companies changed or went out into the field, the dependents moved in with their menfolk, and now it was impossible to distinguish the camp from the village.

Two Strike Force companies were stationed out at the FOB. Two more were on a long-range patrol, sweeping up Highlanders who were no doubt surprised to learn that they were "refugees" who needed to be brought back to enjoy one of the government's Strategic Hamlets. (Back in Pleiku a few weeks later, I visited one of these fortified settlements, built at the order of the late President Diem. An American USAID worker whose room I shared at the Bachelor Officers Quarters called them an "outrage to human decency," and that was certainly true of the one I saw.)

So just one company — about 175 men, somewhat larger than the Strike Force devised by Dave Nuttle — now stayed at Buon Beng as a reserve force, and they too spent much of their time on patrols and ambushes. A week earlier, Captain Judge told me, Cowboy had learned through his intelligence network that three Viet Cong propagandists were operating around Cheo Reo. The Strikers tried to ambush them, but the VC always managed to escape. Finally, when Cowboy's spies reported that a propaganda lecture was scheduled for a nearby village, the captain devised a different plan. Thirty Strikers dressed in loincloths, armed themselves with machetes, and drifted into the village in small groups. Meanwhile, the captain and a fully armed platoon waited in the woods nearby. "It would have been hell," the captain laughed, "to explain how I managed to lose thirty men in loincloths."

Only two VC turned up, one a Highlander and the other an ethnic Vietnamese. The undercover Strikers waited patiently through the lecture, then closed in on the propagandists with machetes drawn. "By the time we got in there to rescue him," Captain Judge said, "the Vietnamese VC was pretty badly cut up. The Montagnard was just bruised a bit around the head and shoulders." Indeed, the hacked-up prisoner had to be evacuated to Pleiku by helicopter for medical treatment. There was much unhappiness in higher headquarters about this outcome, and now Captain Judge had been summoned to Saigon to explain how it had come about.

The captain told me that there were a thousand Viet Cong to the east of Buon Beng and nearly as many to the north, plus uncounted numbers moving through. (Many of them, in the summer of 1964, were actually North Vietnamese regulars, preparing for a big offensive the following year.) This wild, mountainous region was a major infiltration route. A squad of Buon Beng Strikers had set an ambush recently, only to have the terrifying experience of watching a column march past their position for two hours and thirty minutes. The Strikers didn't shoot. Indeed, they scarcely dared to breath. Once, in a similar situation, a man had coughed and nearly cost the lives of an entire platoon. Now the men were issued the cough medicine called "GI Gin" when they went on a night patrol.

"I've given strict orders to my sergeants, especially the younger ones, that they're not to fight when they're outgunned," Captain Judge said. "Communications are too uncertain in the mountains." When communications were uncertain, so was the prospect of reinforcement, so a Strike Force unit operated essentially on its own.

Captain Judge had joined the US Army in 1949. He'd served in Japan as an enlisted man, from which pleasant billet he was sent to Korea with the 1st Cavalry Division to help repel the Communist invasion in the summer of 1950. Afterward, he'd earned the gold bars of a second lieutenant. Like most officers up from the ranks, his days in the army seemed to be numbered. He expected to be "riffed" — subject to a "reduction in force" — after twenty years of service. He'd still be in his thirties when he was forced to retire. I asked him what he planned to do next, and he said: "That's a damned good question."

Taking the Bad with the Good

OBEDIENT TO Major Buck's wishes, I moved out to the FOB as soon as I could hitch a ride. I got my chance on Saturday, after two days of exploring Buon Beng and Cheo Reo. A young Green Beret — unusually, he was a private first class — was taking a company out to relieve one that had been there for a while. I packed my gear and went along.

The convoy consisted of three big "deuce and a half" trucks, so named because they could carry two and a half tons of cargo, plus a three-quarter-ton truck to lead the column and another to bring up the rear. Each of the smaller vehicles had a .30-caliber machine gun mounted behind the driver. The PFC put himself and me in the cab of a deuce and a half. "It's better to swallow dust than to be out front," he said. "If the road is mined, the guys in the three-quarter-ton will be the first to know about it."

The road took us southeast along a winding river, the Song Ba. The countryside was wild and beautiful, rather as I imagined Africa to be, with herds of neat, fat goats fleeing from the thunder of our convoy. Highlanders in loincloths (the women wore wrap-around skirts but were bare-chested like the men) halted beside the road to watch us pass. Some waved and grinned, others just stared. Most carried large wicker baskets, like knapsacks, with carved legs to keep the contents dry when they were put down.

After half an hour, we began to climb a mountain. Choking from the dust swept up by the three-quarter-ton, we mounted higher and higher on curves that turned back on each other like Christmas candy. The mountain rose on one side and fell away on the other. At each turn, short stakes kept the gravel from washing away, but would scarcely have hindered our truck from plunging to the river far below. "I've been over this route about twenty times," said the Green Beret, "and I still pucker up whenever I go through the pass."

It was certainly a fine spot for an ambush. But the most famous battle in this province didn't take place here but on the low ground a few kilometers beyond. We passed the spot about fifteen minutes after coming down to earth again. It was marked by a small white obelisk with an inscription in French and Vietnamese and, more grimly, the rusting carcasses of two Ford-built M-8 armored cars. This was the spot where Group Mobile 100 — with 3,500 men, the equivalent of an American regimental combat team — had its first serious encounter with the Viet Minh, in January 1954.

Major Buck's notion of the ideal Strike Force base was a rough encampment on the right side of the road, some twenty-five kilometers from Cheo Reo. The mountain blocked radio communication between it and Buon Beng, so the men didn't know we were coming. When they heard our engines, two Americans spilled out of the headquarters tent, buttoning their fatigue shirts for fear we might be carrying the major on a surprise inspection tour. They had also donned the regulation Green Beret, but pulled it off when they realized the major wasn't with us. In the field, the favored headgear was a GI baseball cap or a broad brimmed hat like the one Cowboy wore, or that I'd had tailored to my measure soon after arriving in Saigon.

The trucks remained just long enough to swap one company for another, then roared away, leaving me with Russ Brooks and Mike Holland. Each was a specialist fourth class, the equivalent of a three-stripe sergeant. Russ was a small, bony man with a backwoods drawl. Mike was tall and red-haired, with the sunburn affliction of most red-haired people, and wearing plastic-rimmed, Army issue glasses. They were in their twenties and married, like most of the American soldiers I'd met in Vietnam. Mike was a bit older, having served ten years in the Marine Corps before moving to the Army. He was the A Team's second medic, while Russ was a weapons specialist.

The FOB was a desolate place, almost bare of vegetation. A Civil Guard battalion — Highlanders commanded by Vietnamese officers — had formerly occupied this camp, but had been evicted by the Viet Cong. So the Strikers cut down the trees, to get a clear field of fire. They slept in pup-tents fashioned from US Army ponchos, while a green canvas squad tent served as an orderly room and sleeping quarters for the Americans. A flagpole supported a yellow and red Vietnamese flag, hanging limp in the noonday sun. If anything, the place was hotter than Buon Beng.

Russ would be leading a two-squad ambush that night, and he invited me along. It was rule that, on patrol, an American must be awake at all times; since I was an American, he could therefore look forward to getting a bit of sleep. We set out at five o'clock, down a steep slope behind the FOB. As our headquarters unit, we had Little Cowboy, almost as handsome and as well-dressed as his namesake; Old Man, a square-faced, wrinkled warrior with great holes in his ear-lobes who was the senior noncom in Company Five; and two Strikers with a PRC-10 radio slung from a pole between them. (It weighed thirty pounds with handset, antenna, and spare batteries, in addition to which they had to carry their own weapons and personal gear.)

The country through which we marched in the soft light of evening was ever more like the Africa of my imagination: the low, broad trees; the silence, which was absolute except for a crow-like bird that flew overhead, crying *whee-whee-WHEW*; and the flat earth, sparsely covered with grass and cracked from want of rain. We passed charred stilts where huts had been torched by the Strikers or the Viet Cong, and we stepped over the remnants of fallen trees, ghostly shapes the color and texture of charcoal ash.

We walked for two hours, covering eight or nine kilometers, then left one squad at a bend in the river. Our squad crossed over and followed the trail through the high ground on the other side. It was almost dark. We scouted an abandoned village, listened to the voices of fishermen on the river, and, just as night

76

came down, set our own ambush at another river crossing. The men scattered in groups of two, one to stay awake while the other slept.

Little Cowboy produced a mosquito net from beneath his splendid hat. Russ and I doused ourselves with insect repellent. Then we settled down for the night. I was armed with a big Colt .45 pistol, which the supply sergeant had pressed upon me as I was leaving Buon Beng, but Russ wasn't satisfied with that. He gave me his AR-15 as a bed-mate, arming himself with the M-79 grenade launcher that Sergeant Old Man had been carrying. The M-79 was new since my Army days, a shotgun-like affair that fired a 40 mm missile several hundred meters. The Americans called it the "Blooper."

That was the longest night I've ever spent, and I became desperate for a cigarette. I'd quit smoking a year or two earlier, but had recidivated while trekking through the Mekong Delta, seduced by the Lucky Strike five-pack in each C ration box. Fortunately I'd brought along a can of fruitcake, and toward two o'clock I shared it with Russ, the most welcome meal I'd eaten in weeks.

As dawn came on, the patrol reassembled itself into the faces I'd set out with the day before. Cigarettes were lit, some of them American but mostly the cone-shaped cigars that the Highlanders rolled from tobacco and a scrap of paper, or a tobacco leaf if they had no paper. They were issued four leaves a day. Some Strikers chewed them, some smoked them in pipes that were almost straight from bowl to bit, and others fashioned them into cigarettes. (This was a rather casual era in Vietnam. Later, cigarettes and insect repellent would be banned on excursions into Indian Country.)

We made quick work of marching back to the FOB for breakfast, not at all disappointed that our ambush had been a bust. Most ambushes were, but they served a purpose anyhow, keeping the Viet Cong from operating in the open.

That afternoon we had a bit of target practice — Russ, Mike, Old Man, and I. We fired grenades from the Blooper against a tuft of grass on the other side of the Song Ba. Only Old Man was able to hit the target, and he was immensely proud of himself. Then we fired our various sidearms. I emptied a clip from the Colt .45 at a grenade casing twenty meters away, and couldn't come within a meter of it. Finally, Old Man produced a crossbow.

The Highland bow was a beautiful thing, made of what looked like mahogany, with an ivory trigger, a vine for a string, and arrows fashioned from bamboo. The tip had been sharpened, hardened in a fire, and contaminated with human shit or the sap from a poisonous plant. Old Man set up a C ration can, stepped back fifty paces, and fired an arrow at his target. It not only hit the can, but pierced it and stuck out six inches on the other side, as he showed me with a big, sweet smile.

We came back to find that a three-quarter-ton had pulled in from Buon Beng, bringing word that a big operation was in the offing. I could move out with

Brooks and Holland tomorrow morning, or I could return to the base camp and go with the main force. I elected to go back.

We reached Buon Beng in time for lunch. Captain Swain explained that tomorrow's mission was the start of a twenty-day operation called "Quyet Thang 404." Six battalions were taking part — the equivalent of a regiment! The Buon Beng Strikers would make a forced march tomorrow, to be in position next day to support ARVN Rangers coming in by helicopter. Happy Rangers, who did not have to walk to war!

I packed my plastic poncho, a sweater for night wear, toothbrush, compass, first-aid kit, four packs of Lucky Strikes, a quart of water plus an empty water bag, five cans of C rations, and a jackknife. I also had my trusty P-38 can opener on a chain around my neck, the lightest and most useful device the US Army ever devised. Then there were the tools of my trade: notebook, two ballpoint pens, camera, and six rolls of film. Altogether, about twelve pounds, or less than what the BAR and mortar crews would be carrying in weaponry alone.

That done, I went to the supply room to return the Colt. The supply sergeant was happy to take it back, but wanted me to swap it for his own sidearm, a .38-caliber revolver weighing half as much. I managed to persuade him that as a non-combatant I was *supposed* to travel unarmed.

~ ~ ~

Captain Swain gave us a formal briefing that night. Our Strike Force would consist of Company One from

Buon Beng and Company Five from the FOB, three hundred men under the command of eight Americans, plus their Vietnamese shadows from the LLDB. We'd march east from Phouc An, the district headquarters, on Monday morning. Toward evening, Company One would swing north while Five took a southerly route. On Tuesday, after supporting the helicopter assault, each company would divide into sections – seventy-five Strikers and two Americans in each. Finally, on Thursday, we'd reassemble at a village called Tan Hoa. We would thus complete a four-pronged sweep, through a mountainous circle about twenty-five kilometers in diameter.

"We will capture or destroy all VC in the area," said Walter Swain in his briefing-room voice. Clearly he was pleased that this operation was kicking off while Captain Judge was in Saigon apologizing for the cut-up Viet Cong. "We will police up any refugees we find. We will destroy houses, villages, crops, and all livestock except cows." The reprieve for cows got a laugh from the Americans. It was a Vietnamese stipulation, therefore incomprehensible.

We were up at five, and by seven o'clock we were loaded into trucks and moving down the familiar road – Route 7, it was called – over the mountain and past the white obelisk where Group Mobile 100 had been ambushed. We reached the FOB at eight o'clock, and I climbed down, along with the captain, Coffee and his two-man radio team, and Cowboy. The trucks continued to Phouc An with Company One and the four Americans who would lead it. The rest of us waited for the trucks to return. Captain Swain would lead one section of Company Five, with Coffee and Cowboy. Russ Brooks and Mike Holland would lead the second section with the help of Old Man.

The trucks were back in half an hour, and we climbed aboard for the dusty drive down to Phouc An and the valley beyond. When we left Route 7, we shouldered our packs and set off down a trail. The walking was easy, if hot, and Captain Swain set a brisk pace. He had an odd gait: his left foot turned slightly outward and his right foot turned inward, so that he seemed to be walking a bit sideways, like a crab. We were now in Indian Country, so we had a flanking squad in the woods to left and right. There were traces of war all along the trail: empty grenade casings, propaganda leaflets faded by the sun, and finally and most grimly the bodies of two Viet Cong, killed by an ambush two days earlier. They were nearly skeletons already, the bones scattered by animals and yellowed by the sun. The stench was awful, and the Highlanders broke into a run as they passed the bodies.

Captain Swain told me that the two VC had been unarmed but carrying large quantities of ammunition. They'd probably hidden their weapons somewhere and gone into Phouc An to buy ammo from the Civil Guard soldiers stationed there, only to run into a Strike Force ambush on the return trip.

We caught up with the lead company at noon, and the Strikers settled down to cook rice for two meals, since we wouldn't be allowed to build fires tonight. The Americans rested. C rations weren't very appetizing at high noon in the tropics, but they were light, while a Striker consumed a pound of rice at each meal. And C's could be heated in a few minutes, or eaten cold if need be. The Strikers took twenty minutes to cook the first batch of rice, fifteen minutes to eat it, and another twenty minutes to cook the rice they'd eat cold tonight.

We were treading on Company One's heels when the noon break was over, so we passed through and took the lead. We were moving much faster than the ARVN troops I'd accompanied in the Mekong Delta, the breaks were shorter, the sun was directly overhead, and I had only the one quart of water in my metal canteen. Happily our route took us across the Song Ba, so I could splash water on my head and fill the two-quart Army water bag I'd bought at the black market in Saigon. I couldn't quench my thirst, however, because the iodine tablets required fifteen minutes to work their magic, and by then we were on the march again. Three quarts I got at the river, and three quarts were all I'd have until some time tomorrow.

I had, by this time, become friendly with Cowboy — had become quite fond of him, in fact. A young man seldom frets about being killed, but I did consider the possibility I might be taken prisoner. I decided that, if bad came to worst, I'd cook up this story with Cowboy: I was an American writer, researching the story of the National Liberation forces, and he worked for me rather than for the Strike Force. I didn't exactly love him like a brother, as Jim Morris had done, but I was perfectly willing to trust my freedom to him. In retrospect, I suppose that was an error of judgment.

We marched until seven o'clock, then sank to the ground in a clearing, just as twilight was coming down. I opened a can of C ration beef and potatoes and managed to eat half of it, giving the rest to the ever-hungry Russ Brooks. I stuffed my hat with grass to serve as a pillow, spread out my poncho, anointed myself with mosquito repellent, and went to sleep with my hands tucked between my thighs. The repellent would soon wear off, but after two months in Vietnam I was more or less immune to mosquito bites. The thirst bothered me, though. I awoke every hour or two, drank some water, and fell back to sleep, still thirsty.

We were up at five and moved out as soon as we could see our feet. Our two companies now parted. We made for a camel-saddle ridge that separated yesterday's valley from the one we'd sweep today. We reached the high ground at seven-thirty, and at eight o'clock we heard the first helicopter: a droning, fluttering noise beyond the mountain to our left. The Strikers had been issued squares of blaze orange cloth. They now tied these brilliant banners to their packs, or draped them over their heads like kerchiefs, to identify us as friendly forces to the helicopter gunships that would be roving overhead and looking for someone to kill.

We heard the thunder of rockets, followed by the rattle of machineguns, but could see nothing of the helicopter assault. When the firing stopped, we moved down the southern slope along a dry, rocky riverbed.

The slope was steep, the troops behind were rolling rocks down on us, and if we stumbled we couldn't just grab a convenient branch. It might have been a bramble bush, or one of those curious trees whose carbuncular surface was covered with poisonous thorns — the poison often used by the Highlanders on their arrows and on punji sticks.

At the bottom, we moved into the sun. There was mortar fire to our left, and the rattle of burning bamboo: once again Captain Swain's section had moved into the vanguard. We crossed a burned-off area, climbed a small hill, and went down into a wide valley. We saw neither friend nor enemy. That was all right. We were the blocking force, in case the Viet Cong chose to escape over the mountains — if there were any VC.

Here Company Five itself divided. I elected to go with the section led by Russ Brooks and Mike Holland and, more discreetly, by a Vietnamese lieutenant and noncom of the LLDB. We also had Old Man with us, and it was he who served as Mike's spokesman with the Strikers. He also protected the Americans: more than once I felt his soft touch on my arm, and with a big grin he would warn me of punji sticks or a thorn bush. And it was he who found a water hole — a gray, evil looking pool — where we filled our canteens.

We were the most southerly sweep. Like Sherman marching through Georgia, we burned everything we saw, and our path was marked by billows of gray smoke and the snap of burning bamboo, like a rear-guard battle following us wherever we went.

At one point, Mike got into an argument with the LLDB officer. Mike got red in the face and shook his fist at the lieutenant, who unlike the Americans chose to wear his beret into the field. This astonishing scene — a buck sergeant physically threatening an officer — ended with the two Vietnamese moving to the rear of the column with sullen faces. If that had been a US Army officer, Mike would have ended his career on the rock pile at Fort Leavenworth.

This was wildly at odds with the US Army's understanding of how an A Team functioned. On paper, the LLDB ran the show, with the Americans offering suggestions from time to time. "On patrol, however," as an Army historian admitted, "the Vietnamese Special Forces often abdicated this role, with command then going to the US Special Forces by default." But from what I saw, not only in the Highlands but also at CIDG camps in the Mekong Delta, this was actually standard operating procedure: the Green Berets ran the show.

~ ~ ~

The valley narrowed around us, as if we were walking into the mouth of a funnel, and the air became ever more still and hot. I pitied the Strikers, many of them carrying mortars or BARs as well as packs far heavier than mine, but even more I pitied myself. At one point Russ Brooks confessed that he was tiring. I reminded him that the Green Berets were supposed to be the toughest soldiers in the world. "Maybe so," he said, "but we get tired just like anybody else." When it came to water, he was actually in worse shape than I. Somehow he'd missed the word about carrying extra water; he'd left the FOB with only his one quart metal canteen, which was now dry. I gave him a drink from my mine.

At three o'clock we reached the end of the valley, where it turned into a dry riverbed coming down from the mountains. We were now in the forest. We climbed a trail beneath the trees, and never was shade more welcome. It was a claustrophobic spot, however, as if from an open avenue we'd come into a dark alley, unable to see more than ten feet to either side. The land sloped away to the right; we were following a trail on the left bank of the gully.

Then Mike spotted three young men, high up the slope. They were cooking dinner behind the boulders that were our afternoon's objective. "VC," he whispered, studying them through his binoculars. He sent a squad of Strikers down into the ravine without their packs, to circle around and approach the high ground from the other side. Russ meanwhile took aim with his AR-15. We tried to be quiet, but down the line a Striker was coughing, and I could hear the snap and rustle of bushes as our flanking squad went through the gully. Mike pushed the binoculars into my hand. "They'll hear us," he whispered. "Keep an eye on them and tell me what they're doing." Then he propped his rifle on his knee.

I was supposed to write about the Green Berets, not serve as their target spotter, but I was certainly interested in seeing an actual Viet Cong guerrilla. The man who leaped into my vision wore a black shirt and trousers, and his face was young and alert beneath a crown of thick black hair. He was looking down into the gully where our flanking squad was moving. I reported this to Mike. Then the young guerrilla turned as if to move away, and I reported this as well.

"Do I shoot?" Russ whispered. It was a dilemma: five hundred meters uphill was an impossibly difficult shot, but if they waited they might lose the quarry altogether. Then Mike decided for both of them: he fired. The AR-15 is a quiet weapon, and the shot was like the sound of a branch breaking. There was a pause before Russ fired his first round. "Damn it, Mike," he wailed. "I had him in my sights, and I lost him!"

We took off at a run, with the adrenalin pumping – up, up, scrambling on hands and knees when we had to. But our quarry had flown when we reached the boulders. We found three white scars on the rock face, all low by at least two feet, but damned good shooting at that distance and angle.

We spent the night there on the ledge. For dinner I ate a C-ration can of fruitcake, which required a quart of water for me to wash down. It was my first food since a few spoonfuls of beef and potatoes twenty-four hours earlier. Nevertheless, I awoke on Wednesday feeling fresh enough to march, though I did give Russ my metal canteen. He needed the extra water, and I was glad to get rid of the weight.

We spent the morning slabbing a mountainside on a compass course, in and out of gullies whose existence had been ignored by the French cartographers who'd drawn our maps. When we reached the summit at noon, the world seemed good again. Green mountains tumbled away on all sides, no different than the hills of home, and except for the heat and the punji sticks we might have been tramping the Appalachian Trail from Georgia to Maine.

At three o'clock we reached the river that was supposed to lead us to Tan Hoa, where the Buon Beng companies would come together. Alas, the river was dry. Still, we took a break while the Strikers cooked their noontime rice with whatever water remained to them. I ate a can of chopped ham and eggs, soft as baby food, and drank the last ounce in my water bag. Russ had finished his two quarts as well.

As soon as we moved out, we met Captain Swain's section. They had nearly fifty refugees with them: an old woman with a wicker pack that must have weighed seventy-five pounds; a blind boy who clung to the bottom of his mother's pack and screamed in terror when he lost hold of it, scrambling through a forest he couldn't see on a mission he couldn't comprehend; a girl about six years old, carrying her baby brother, who was almost as big as she; and another girl with runny eyes and a swarm of flies that kept dodging into them.

"They told Cowboy they left their village when they heard the shooting yesterday morning," the captain told us. "They've had no food since then, and no water since last night. There was an old woman with them; she moved about an inch a minute. We had to leave her." He shrugged. "She'll die," he said.

We followed a compass line through the woods — gullies, ridges, bramble bushes. The map promised a trail, and at five o'clock Captain Swain called a break and sent a search party down into the gully to look for it, and that was how we finally found water. There was a clear, beautiful pool of it between two stone-dry stretches of riverbed. Here I discovered a major disadvantage of the water bag: I had to borrow Captain Swain's metal canteen, to use as a dipper to fill the bag. "What happened to your canteen?" he asked.

"I gave it to Russ. He was at the FOB and didn't get the word about carrying extra water."

"He fucked up," Captain Swain said — the Army's all-purpose dismissal of a personal misfortune.

"You're not very sympathetic," I said.

He laughed. "Well, that's the worst part of a forced march," he said. "It's not your own exhaustion — hell, you can always put one foot in front of the other, if you have to — but the way you lose sympathy for the men around you. If the guy next to you falls down, you don't help him up."

Then he relented and told how he himself had once fucked up. Out on patrol, he'd drunk deep from his water bag, then set it down while he whittled kindling for a fire. Done with the knife, he spun it for fun into the ground — right through the bag. "I tell you," he said, "there's no sadder sight in all the world, than watching tomorrow's water making a dark spot on the ground."

As darkness came down, we reached an open field, and Captain Swain announced that we'd found Tan

Hoa. I didn't see a village, but I was too tired to wonder. I laid down my bit of plastic, then myself; I put the bush hat over my face, tucked my hands between my thighs, and slept.

In the tropics, dawn and dusk come very quickly, and at about the same hour, seven o'clock. I'd found this disconcerting at first, but now it seemed in the nature of things, as did the entire enterprise — policing up refugees, burning the occasional hut, marching ten hours a day with the Strikers and the Green Berets. I admired Captain Swain, I was fond of Russ Brooks and Mike Holland, and I *enjoyed* Cowboy. We grinned whenever we met, though I don't remember ever actually having a conversation with him.

John McPhee once wrote about looking for bear in arctic Alaska, and how he came to feel at home in that alien climate, with companions who in the ordinary course of life he'd never have met. Searching for a word to describe the change that had come over him, he hit upon *incorporated*. "To be there," he wrote, "was to be incorporated, in however small a measure, into [the bear's] substance — his country." In just that way, I had been incorporated into the Highlands, and into the Vietnam War. I regret to say that I loved it — the land, the people and, yes, the war.

~ ~ ~

In the morning, Mike held sick call for the refugees. Then we moved out. After an hour's march, we crossed a river and reached a dirt road between the mountains. Here, at an open place near the river, was the actual site of Tan Hoa, and here we stopped to

90

cook. It was a bright, beautiful morning, and for the first time since leaving Buon Beng I was actually hungry. I bartered a Lucky Strike for a can of cooked rice, into which I mixed the contents of a C-ration can of meat and noodles, for a fine casserole.

Captain Swain set up a command post on a small, tree-shaded hill, where there were still traces of the fortifications that had once protected Tan Hoa. On the southern slope, I inspected a Gallic cross and four neat French graves, undisturbed by the ten years that had elapsed between their war and ours. The little cemetery had a stone border, now overgrown by grass. I remembered the epitaph for King Leonidas and his followers who died to hold the pass at Thermopylae against an invading Persian army: *Go, stranger, and tell the Spartans / that we lie here in obedience to their laws.* According to John Ruskin, those were the noblest words ever written by man. I wondered if the four Frenchmen buried here would have agreed.

When we hoisted our packs to leave this pleasant place, we heard a rifle shot. Captain Swain ran to the crown of the hill with his binoculars. He reported that he saw a lone man in the field, five hundred meters from us, with an infantry rifle in his hand and a just-killed deer on his shoulder.

Poor, misguided Viet Cong! One moment he was gloating over his kill; the next moment, mortar shells were exploding around him and three hundred Strikers were running across the field to bring him down. But he got away. Our only haul was the deer, plus two women who were suspiciously close to the carcass when we found it. They were ethnic Vietnamese, not Highlanders, with conical hats and black pajamas. Cowboy snapped and snarled at them, but they claimed to know nothing about the deer hunter.

The bullying bothered me, and I must have showed it. "You've got to take the bad with the good," Captain Swain reminded me. "And Cowboy is a good interpreter."

We made a barbecue pit from one of the old French fighting holes, and we grilled the venison on sharpened sticks. It was tough and sweet. Then we again prepared to move out.

Minutes after we cleared the area, a mortar shell exploded on our picnic site. Apparently the Viet Cong were bivouacked a kilometer away, and were now taking revenge for the theft of their venison and two of their women. We'd lost half the morning in cooking, chasing, and cooking again, and it was now noon, so we let them have the last word.

Portfolio: The Strikers at War

Duc Co camp was on Highway 19 between Pleiku and Cambodia, so it protected the provincial capital and enabled the Strikers to intercept troops coming from North Vietnam by way of the Ho Chi Minh Trail. Rather than a defended village like Buon Enao, Duc Co was a fort in its own right, and a symbol of the evolution of the Civilian Irregular Defense Group. Cowboy was an interpreter here, and the friend and bodyguard of Captain Johnnie Corns, the Special Forces commander. (US government)

Did you ever see such joy on a human face, or such a cocky posture? In a little ceremony at Buon Beng, Jim Morris awarded US Army airborne wings to Cowboy (on the left) and Kpa Doh. Sergeant Ken Miller towers over the two Highlanders. The white name tag and white tee-shirt were standard for the time, but I took the precaution of muddying mine.
(Jim Morris)

The Green Berets at Buon Beng were the first to hear of a planned Strike Force uprising. Cowboy tipped off the Americans, who alerted Major Buck in Pleiku. From left: Captain McCulloch, Cowboy with his hands on his pistol belt, two unidentified FULRO activists, Nay Luett in jacket and tie, Kpa Doh, and the major. Officials in Saigon scoffed at the warning. (Crews McCulloch)

A US Army "deuce-and-a-half" (two-and-one-half-ton truck) loaded with Strike Force troopers ready to move out on a patrol from Buon Beng. The Strikers are wearing colored scarfs to mark them as friendly troops in case there are US Army helicopters or Vietnamese air force fighter planes prowling overhead. (Michael Holland)

A company of Buon Beng Strikers in June 1964. Cowboy is on the left, leading the column with all the grace of a Douglas MacArthur. On the right is Captain Swain, cradling his Colt AR-15. Before setting out, he warned us to dress like the Strikers, so as not to be targeted by a sniper. He was not very successful in following the advice. (Daniel Ford)

Not long after reaching Tan Hoa, we heard a shot, and Captain Swain spotted a hunter with the deer he had just killed. Three hundred Strikers set out to capture him, firing rifles and the occasional mortar shell, but I think everyone was laughing too hard to hit anything. He got away, but we captured the deer and some women in conical hats, whom Cowboy is escorting at right. That's a French grave in the foreground, and radioman Charles Coffing just beyond. After we roasted and ate the deer, a mortar shell exploded nearby, so we called the battle a draw and left Tan Hoa to the enemy. (Daniel Ford)

No More 'Terry and the Pirates'

THE REFUGEES couldn't keep up. At the three o'clock break, the old woman with the huge pack caught up with us and settled in the road beside Captain Swain. "Sir," Cowboy translated, "the refugees request food."

"Tell her there isn't any," the captain said. "Tell her there will be food and water where we stop tonight."

I dug into my pack and took out three bits of venison left over from our barbecue. I gave them to the old woman, who grinned and held the meat tightly in her hand. She had no teeth, but could have sucked on it with pleasure, so she must have been saving it for her family.

Then we heard the *whup-whup* of a Huey's rotor blades. In the course of trying to contact it — "Army aircraft, Army aircraft, this is Blaze, Blaze; do you have any traffic for this station?" — Coffee accidentally reached Major Buck, on the ground about three kilometers from us. Captain Swain took the handset and explained the plight of our refugees. Could he split the company? He'd bring his section to join the major, while Russ Brooks and Mike Holland stayed with the refugees. We were supposed to return this way tomorrow, and there was little point in marching these poor people up the mountain, only to turn them around and march them down again.

"Negative," said the major.

Russ groaned, and I groaned with him. There was nothing I'd rather have done than remain in that shady spot until Thursday, with a river not far away. But Six Eight Baseball Glove wanted us to join him, and he was the major, so we hoisted our packs and moved out into the sun.

The next hour was the hardest of the patrol. Captain Swain had been inspired by the major's voice, it seemed, and determined to show how fast he could bring a company home. We stepped out like demons. We crossed a boggy field of saw grass, then climbed a thirty-degree slope that seemed to have no end. We passed the spot where the major's party had eaten lunch yesterday: empty cans that had held C rations for the Americans and sardines for the Vietnamese, and a crumpled Lucky Strike pack. We stopped for nothing, and we were on the high, grassy plateau at the summit exactly one hour after Captain Swain had talked to the major.

But Six Eight Baseball Glove wasn't there to admire our speed. Just as we broke into the clearing, we heard the fluttering noise of Huey helicopters, taking off with him and his party.

A company of ARVN Rangers was waiting for us at the far end of the plateau — cheerful Highlanders in red berets and red scarves, with their Vietnamese officers. "Where's the major?" Captain Swain asked, shaking hands with the two American advisors with the Rangers.

"He left," said the taller of the two. "He spent two

days in the field, and he's had the ass."

Then, like a miracle in the shape of an olive green dragonfly, a Huey came over the plateau, circled down to our clearing, and alighted. I had no idea where it had come from, why it had landed, or whither it was bound. Nevertheless I climbed aboard. I buckled myself into the rear bench seat, to make it more difficult for anybody to kick me off. Russ came over to say goodbye and return my metal canteen. I emptied my water bag into his canteen. We shook hands, and I promised to send photographs of our excursion to his wife on Okinawa.

The helicopter was airborne seconds later, flying effortlessly over the mountains I'd traversed with such difficulty. It took me to the Special Forces camp at Dong Tre, near the coast, and there it abandoned me while it took rice and blankets to the refugees.

The first person I saw at Dong Tre was Six Eight Baseball Glove himself. We were equally astonished. "Outstanding!" the major cried, when I told him I'd been out in the field with the Buon Beng Strikers. I took advantage of his momentary admiration to borrow his razor, soap, and toothpaste, and I went down to the shower room to scrub off the filth of four days in the field.

While I was washing, a young fool of a captain came into the shower room, dragging one of those oversized, metal-framed rucksacks that Green Berets called "the Mountain." He introduced himself. (In *Incident at Muc Wa*, he would become Captain Olivetti, a name borrowed from my typewriter.) He was from the B Team in Pleiku, and he'd been with the major's party yesterday and today. Those were his C ration cans and Lucky Strike pack on the trail this afternoon.

I asked if he had taken that monster rucksack into the mountains with him. "Oh yes," he assured me. "Creature comforts are very important in the field." I was too tired to inquire what sort of comforts he was carrying — a jungle hammock, probably, or an air mattress. Certainly I saw one of those weighty US Army ponchos, rolled at the top of his pack. No field soldier carried a GI poncho in Vietnam. If it rained, the poncho wouldn't keep him dry (he'd sweat beneath it), and anyhow he'd soon dry off in the sun. And as a ground cloth for sleeping, a strip of plastic serves the same purpose at one tenth the weight.

The captain had a tale of woe. A helicopter had landed him in the boondocks yesterday, in the wrong clearing, and without a map. Only great good luck had enabled him to catch up with Major Buck and his party. Of course, he said, he wasn't worried about being alone in the forest, except for the fact that he'd just bought a Rolex. It had galled him to think that the Viet Cong might get his new watch.

~ ~ ~

I never saw Cowboy again, though like Captain Olivetti he served me well in the novel that came out of Quyet Thang 404. In the movie, *Go Tell the Spartans*, he was played, rather savagely, by the Korean-American actor Evan Kim.

Mike Holland tells me that when Captain Judge

came back from Saigon, having explained why prisoners at Buon Beng often came to a bad end, he fired Cowboy, who then got a job at Camp Holloway with the new B Team commander, Major Edwin Brooks. (For all that Captain Judge expected to be riffed after completing thirty years of service, the Vietnam War kept him on active duty. "Wars make young majors," as company-level officers like to say, and so it worked out. He was not only promoted to major, but he eventually retired as a lieutenant colonel — not bad for a man who'd come up from the ranks.)

Though I lost track of Cowboy, I certainly heard about the FULRO rebellion. That September, three thousand Strikers at five camps took up arms against the Saigon government. Buon Beng wasn't among them. The uprising centered on Ban Me Thuot, in the area so successfully pacified by Dave Nuttle, the CIA, and the Green Berets two years before. The rebel Highlanders killed two civilians, fifteen Popular Force militiamen, and twenty-six of their LLDB cadre. At Bu Prang, they tied the LLDB captain to the flagpole and threw the bodies of his men into the latrine. Some Americans were locked up overnight but weren't injured, and at some camps they were able to protect their Vietnamese colleagues. "To kill them, you'll have to kill me first," Captain Vernon Gillespie told the rebellious Rhade at Buon Brieng.

Strikers from three camps then marched on Ban Me Thuot, joined by troops from the FULRO refuge at Camp le Rolland. They failed to capture the town but did occupy some nearby villages. More important, they seized the radio station, from which Y Bham Enoul denounced Vietnamese genocide and demanded autonomy for the Highland provinces. For several days, the FULRO flag flew over the radio station and the "liberated" villages and CIDG camps. General Nguyen Khanh, the junta leader who happened to be prime minister at the time, made two flying visits to Ban Me Thuot to negotiate a settlement. (He chose not to spend the night.) On the second day, he lost his temper and ordered ARVN troops to storm the camp at Buon Sa Par, but a quick-thinking American colonel headed off the assault by himself freeing the LLDB hostages.

General Khanh pledged not to punish the rebels, who then stacked their weapons and let the ARVN enter their camps. Hundreds of them — perhaps a thousand or more — moved across the border to Camp le Rolland.

Cowboy and Nay Luett were among the delegates who came to Pleiku in October for a parley at the Phoenix Officers Club. Gerald Hickey, who had worked in Vietnam for nearly ten years, recalled that the FULRO delegates were "dressed in tailored suits with white shirts and dark ties" — a turnout that, try as I will, I cannot imagine Cowboy wearing. He was indeed a man of many talents.

General Khanh agreed to almost all of the rebel demands except their plan for a Highlander army of 25,000-50,000 men, fighting under the FULRO flag. The concessions were generous, though few would be honored by Saigon, and all five of the rebel camps would be closed within a year. There were some minor improvements: the Rhade law court was reinstated, and the Rhade language would again taught be in school.

Despairing that negotiations would bring any serious improvement in the Highlanders' lot, Y Bham Enoul moved to Camp le Rolland with his staff. If five years in prison had not radicalized him, General Khanh's duplicity did the trick. There was no longer a militant and a peaceful wing of the independence movement, but only differing degrees of militance. In March 1965, Y Bham traveled to Phnom Penh to take part in a conference sponsored by Norodom Sihanouk, the former king, now the Cambodian head of state. In the Vietnamese civil war, he favored the Communists in Hanoi over the generals (and Americans!) in Saigon, so he was happy to help FULRO cause trouble for them.

In Saigon, meanwhile, the trim and flashy air force chief, General Nguyen Cao Ky, deposed General Khanh and became prime minister in his place, which somewhat brightened the Highlanders' situation. For the first time, the government got a department devoted to ethnic minorities, with Nay Luett and Paul Nur on its staff, and six Highlanders were elected to the National Assembly.

~ ~ ~

It was probably no accident that the Phnom Penh conference coincided with Hanoi's next attempt to cut South Vietnam in two. The men who had come down the Ho Chi Minh Trail in the early years were mostly southern veterans from the war against the French, who had gone north after the partition in 1954. They belonged to the Viet Cong 338th Division which, though trained and armed in the North, did have some claim to be an indigenous force. This was now changing. In 1964, three full regiments of the PAVN — People's Army of [North] Vietnam — came down the trail to reinforce and sometimes absorb the Viet Cong units operating in the Highlands. In the summer of 1965, they launched an offensive to isolate the provincial capitals by closing the roads leading to them.

At Cheo Reo, the Buon Beng camp was about to be closed down in favor of a new location at Phu Tuc. (I don't think this was the FOB where I'd spent a few days the year before, but some distance farther along Route 7.) The splendidly named Captain Fleming Bukey Brainerd III and his Detachment A-224 came into the country toward the end of April and established themselves at Phu Tuc on May 21. Five days later, the Viet Cong attacked the nearby village of Buon Mroc, driving out the Popular Force platoon defending it. The district chief sent a Regional Force company to retake the village. On paper, these were conventional military units, but the Ruff Puffs were really just militia, wearing civilian clothes and carrying bolt-action rifles left behind by the French.

Before the Ruffs reached Buon Mroc, they were ambushed and had to radio for reinforcement. Captain Brainerd answered the call with the Phu Tuc Strikers, but was himself ambushed and forced to call for help. This brought down fighter planes from

Pleiku, along with a helicopter-borne "Eagle Flight" of thirty-odd Highlanders under the command of American Green Berets. In the end, Highway 7 was cleared, but at the cost of Bukey Brainerd, killed by enemy fire.

And so it went through the summer and fall of 1965, as the war increasingly turned into a contest between the US Army and the PAVN. In July the Communists bloodied Cowboy's old stomping ground at Duc Co, between Pleiku and the Cambodian border. They still expected to win the war by slicing through South Vietnam along Highway 19, from Pleiku to the coast. First, of course, they had to control the ground between Cambodia and Pleiku. This led to the US Army's first all-out battle in the Highlands, made famous by the book and the Mel Gibson movie, *We Were Soldiers Once*.

Both sides were shocked by the bloody brawl in the Ia Drang valley. The "airmobile" 1st Cavalry Division discovered that its vaunted mobility worked better in training than in battle, because helicopters wore out and broke down under constant use. And American firepower was largely nullified by the PAVN doctrine of "hold the enemy by the belt" — crowd so close to the Americans that, if they called for artillery support, they would be killing themselves. For their part, the North Vietnamese discovered the awful weight of American bombs, dropped by the ton from eight-engine Boeing B-52s, acquired to drop nuclear bombs on the Soviet Union. Two PAVN regiments were more or less destroyed in the battle for the Ia Drang valley.

FULRO was also heard from at this time. On December 17, Y Bham Enoul led another rebellion, briefly taking control of Ban Me Thuot and two CIDG camps, along with camps in four other provinces. Thirty Vietnamese — a district chief among them — were killed in this second uprising. Though it accomplished nothing, it did show that FULRO was still a force to be reckoned with. Its estimated strength in 1965 was seven thousand troops at Camp le Rolland and elsewhere along the Cambodian border.

From Strike Force to Mike Force

ONE OF GENERAL Khanh's concessions to the rebels was actually honored by the ARVN. For the first time, Highlanders were allowed to become army officers, entering at the grade of *aspirant*. In French service, an aspirant was a probationary officer, a sort of third lieutenant, his status roughly equal to that of a warrant officer in the US Army. During the First Indochina War, Nal Moul had served in the French Colonial Army at that grade, before he joined the Viet Minh.

Cowboy became one of these aspirants. It seems however that he was never paid — always a hazard for an ARVN soldier! — or anyhow not paid enough to satisfy his self-esteem, and he deserted after a year. That apparently suited his superiors just fine, because the ARVN made no effort to bring him back.

He went to the seacoast and became chief interpreter at the Nha Trang Mike force. Though it's often capitalized, "Mike" isn't an acronym, but the thirteenth letter in the phonetic alphabet, as shorthand for "Mobile Strike Force." The euphony of *Mike* and *Strike* no doubt helped make it stick. Its origins could be traced to the Mountain Scouts, financed by the CIA in 1961 and trained by Larry Arritola's comrades from Detachment A-213, and to the Eagle Flight that had proved its worth in opening Route 7 between Cheo

Reo and Phu Tuc.

There were two Mike Force battalions at Nha Trang and one in each of the other military districts. Like the original Eagle Flight, each was manned by motivated, combat-qualified indigenous troops under the direct command of the Green Berets, along with volunteers from the Australian Special Air Service. And like the Mountain Scouts, Mike Force was at home in the forest, able to stay out for up to two months at a time, on rations consisting mostly of rice and a bit of fish.

Meanwhile, the Green Berets themselves were reorganized. Instead of flying in from Okinawa, they were given their own 5th Special Forces Group, based at Nha Trang. (Captain Brainerd's A Team at Phu Tuc was one of the first to come into Vietnam on a "permanent change of station," serving a year-long tour instead of six months.) And the B Teams in the four military regions, like the one at Camp Holloway outside Pleiku, were upgraded to "C" detachments. The US Army has long been famous for its "tail," the scores of clerks and administrators who support each rifleman in the field, but in Vietnam the REMFs (Rear Echelon Mother Fuckers) had become legendary in quantity.

~ ~ ~

That first Mike Force at Nha Trang was formed in November 1965 from a company of ethnic Chinese Strikers called the Nung. A Green Beret veteran, "Donald H.," described how it grew:

"After a period of several months permission was

requested and received to begin recruiting Montagnards from the indigenous tribal groups in the Highlands of South Vietnam. SFC Manfred Baier, senior medic, was dispatched immediately to Ban Me Thuot. . . . Baier was successful in finding some of his old Montagnard comrades [from an earlier tour] and after several meetings with the leadership of the Montagnard secret government (FULRO) he was rewarded with a force of 220 Rhade Montagnards. . . . He immediately informed his CO of the success of his mission. Orders were cut & he began to have the new recruits shuttled to Nha Trang from Ban Me Thuot by C-123 aircraft. . . .

"Capt. Carter also sent Sgt Bill Caldwell to Ban Me Thuot on a recruiting mission . . . accompanied by a Montagnard interpreter named Philip and on arrival in the Ban Me Thuot area met another Rhade interpreter named 'Pedro' who subsequently introduced him to a Rhade tribal chief named 'N'yet'. Over the next 2 days Sgt Caldwell and the 2 interpreters were successful in obtaining Chief Nyet's permission to transfer 166 of his tribesmen to Nha Trang for induction into the Mike force."

Philip of course was Cowboy, and "Pedro" must have been Kpa Doh, sometimes called Pardo by the Americans. "N'yet" would have been Nay Luett, who like Cowboy was married to one of the Rcom women. It's amusing to think that, while the Americans believed they were recruiting the Rhade, the Highlanders were actually taking over the Nha Trang Mike Force.

111

Naturally Cowboy continued to recruit for FULRO, for which activity he apparently was fired in 1966. Some Mike Force units were entirely made up of FULRO troops, who contributed ten percent of their pay to the organization. Some of this money no doubt made its way into Cowboy's pockets. The USAID worker Mike Benge thought that, like an executive headhunter, Cowboy charged Mike Force recruits three months' salary in exchange for getting the job. That would have been greater cause for his dismissal from the force.

Or perhaps he simply decided to move on to a larger field of action. The war had changed utterly by this time, and the Highlands with it. Pleiku, Cheo Reo, and Ban Me Thuot had become squalid boom towns, crowded with military vehicles, sleazy bars, "massage parlors," and prostitutes in miniskirts, and surrounded by shantytowns of refugees from the countryside. There were sixteen thousand American servicemen in South Vietnam when I left the country in July 1964; two years later, the head count was nearly half a million. Communist strength was said to be 260,000 including 50,000 North Vietnamese, though I suspect the latter figure was an underestimate.

"By mid 1966," as Gerald Hickey sorrowfully expressed the change, "the Vietnam War had become a tidal wave of death and destruction sweeping unrestrained across South Vietnam."

~ ~ ~

Back in Vietnam the following year, Jim Morris was shocked by the changes. During his first tour in

Vietnam, the war had had "a nice 'Terry and the Pirates' ambiance to it." Yes! That 1930s-1940s comic strip by Milton Caniff captured exactly the thrill I'd experienced in South Vietnam — exotic people, colorful scenery, and just enough danger to make it exciting. Though I always pressed as closely as I could to what passed for the front lines, I was never *frightened* in Vietnam. But when Morris returned a few years later, life was different. "Now," he mused, Vietnam "was full of psychotic commanders who thought they were refighting World War II with helicopters."

He naturally hoped to get an A Team of his own, but as a captain on the brink of becoming a major, he was instead told to command a desk in Pleiku. Lonesome for the old days of romping and stomping, he went looking for his former interpreter and sidekick. By sniffing around, he learned that Cowboy now signed himself "Col. Philip Drouin, Commanding, Dam-Yi Mobile Division of Commando Paratrooper" — a warlord, in short. Indeed, the former interpreter had jumped through five officer grades, from ARVN sub-lieutenant to FULRO colonel, while Morris still wore the silver bars of a captain.

And Kpa Doh was a FULRO major! He was easier to locate, and Morris soon found an opportunity to helicopter down to Ban Me Thuot to meet him. To ensure a welcome, he borrowed a jeep and filled it with medical supplies, bags of rice, and two cases of carbine ammunition. These were unloaded by the bodyguards who lounged about the house, one of many conventional masonry dwellings that mingled with Rhade longhouses in the suburb of Buon Ale A, southwest of town on Route 14. (I call it a suburb rather than a village, because it was thoroughly westernized by this time. It even boasted a Protestant mission, with a chapel and three "Italian villas" for the missionaries.)

Cowboy, it turned out, also lived in Buon Ale A. Gerald Hickey had visited him there, as he wrote in *Free in the Forest*, his study of Highlander culture:

"Philippe lived in a masonry house (considered very expensive for one in his status), and when I visited him he proudly displayed an expensive hi-fi set on which he played rock music. He also had sets of American army fatigues on which Spanish names such as Sanchez and Gonzales had been sewn. On the shoulders were American Special Forces patches. He explained that from time to time he would go to Saigon and pose as an American of Spanish origin (he spoke English with only a slight accent). Philippe also drove around Ban Me Thuot either on a Honda motorcycle . . . or in his new pickup truck (robin egg blue in color). Almost every evening he went to the Darlac II nightclub, frequented by American and Vietnamese military personnel, where he drank scotch whiskey and danced with the Vietnamese hostesses."

He had other favorite nightspots, notably the International Bar and a restaurant called *La Souris Blanche*, the White Mouse. The latter was popular with the owners of coffee and rubber plantations and agents from the French intelligence agency popularly known as the *Deuxième Bureau.*

Cowboy's house, as Jim Morris saw it, had "rattan furniture all over the living room, and more flunkies [than Kpa Doh's], looking more attentive." The music was that of Herb Alpert and the Tijuana Brass, coming from an Akai tape deck that seemed to have one faulty speaker. Rather than Cowboy's wardrobe, Morris noted that house was well equipped with US Army carbines, mortars, machineguns, and "other exotic military stuff."

Cowboy himself was almost unrecognizable with his hair cut short and wearing slacks and a Lacoste jersey. His wife and stepdaughter were still in Cheo Reo — H'un, it seemed, had left him, or he had left her. Gerald Hickey reported that Cowboy had "treated the girl badly, often beating her. . . . Subsequently, [she] had severe mental problems." More specifically, Mike Benge told me that Cowboy had prostituted her: he "ran his own little cathouse there" at Buon Beng. Her father, Nay Moul, tried to confine the young woman in the family longhouse, but from time to time she would escape and wander the roads. More than once, it seems, she was gang-raped by ARVN soldiers.

Such was the dark side of the interpreter whom so many Americans — myself included — had liked and trusted.

~ ~ ~

The Dam-Y Division boasted three thousand troops, so it was really an understrength regiment. Cowboy, Jim Morris learned, was on the payroll of "just about every supersecret military intelligence outfit in

Vietnam, none of whom apparently knew about the others," which may have explained the various uniforms Gerald Hickey had seen around the house.

Mike Benge named SMIAT as one of Cowboy's employers. Though it sounds like something Ian Fleming might have invented, the Special Military Intelligence Activities Team was indeed a US Army outfit, though I find almost nothing about it on the internet. In the Highlands, it apparently operated under the pseudonym of the Field Sociological Survey, based in Buon Ale A, the architecturally and ethnically mixed suburb that was home to Cowboy, Kpa Doh, and Mike Benge. Despite their academic title, the "Survey" personnel lived in what Hickey described as a compound surrounded by a "high fence, guard posts, and spotlights."

If one of Cowboy's employers needed troops for a special project, he would rent a few hundred men for a week or a month, an arrangement that also served to keep the troops in fighting trim and give them a bit of money to send home. Some of these arrangements may have been permanent: Morris later mentions that B-50, the Mike Force unit at the airfield east of Ban Me Thuot, was actually a Dam-Y rent-a-battalion.

Next day, the two men drove out to visit the training camp, with Colonel Drouin at the wheel of Morris's jeep. Cowboy wore a tailored American uniform, complete with holstered revolver, a 1st Cavalry Division patch, and US Army airborne wings, signifying that he had completed the parachute course at Fort Bragg. He hadn't, of course; the wings had been given him at Buon Beng in 1964. Five jumps were needed to qualify for the airborne. Cowboy was now claiming fifty or so, so Morris obligingly got the wings upgraded to senior parachutist.

Cowboy drove east. Once clear of Ban Me Thuot, Morris jacked a cartridge into the chamber of his M-16, the much-improved version of the AR-15 he'd carried during his first tour in Vietnam. He explained the precaution this way: "I don't think Philip would have sold [me] out for money, but there was always the chance he had made friends with the VC during the three years I was away. . . . I felt kind of smug about the fact that Philip and I were each sufficiently professional in our outlooks that we could kill each other if it proved necessary. It seems a strange existence, but I was at home with it and happy."

Morris was much impressed by the Dam-Y Division. Cowboy's soldiers were — well, *soldierly*. They were relaxed but alert, their carbines were clean and oiled, and they saluted their colonel smartly. The village was likewise tidy, and its defenses well maintained. With all the chitchat and nitty-gritty, the reader comes away from *War Story* almost unaware that Morris hasn't given the slightest clue as to where Cowboy's fortress village was located, save that it was east of Ban Me Thuot, toward the coast, but probably no more than fifteen or twenty kilometers. He seemed to have gone out and back the same day, and the roads in the 1960s did not encourage long-distance driving.

~ ~ ~

So Cowboy worked for both FULRO and the Ameri-

117

cans, though it's not clear *which* Americans — Mike Force, Special Forces, CIA, SMIAT, all of them, or perhaps someone else entirely, the *Deuxième Bureau* perhaps. There were many "dark" operations in Southeast Asia at the height of the US involvement, as first President Johnson, then President Nixon, tried to free himself from the tar baby of the Saigon regime. Adopting the tactics used so successfully by the Viet Cong in the early years, the Phoenix Program killed, imprisoned, converted, or otherwise "neutralized" nearly eighty-two thousand VC operatives, real or suspected.

Then there were the Cambodians. As king, prime minister, and head of state, Norodom Sihanouk portrayed himself as a neutralist but favored Hanoi, and he had been a longtime backer of the Highlander independence movement. Many of the Strikers who moved across the border had now become officers in the Cambodian army, including Nay Luett as a major. And Cowboy, remember, had been a French colonial soldier in Cambodia.

It's even possible that he worked for North Vietnam, because he enjoyed the rewards of money and status that came from playing the game in that divided country. And there was so much money to be had! "By 1967," as Stanley Kramer wrote in his superlative history of the war, "a million tons of supplies a month were pouring into Vietnam to sustain the U.S. force — an average of a hundred pounds a day for every American there." Most of those Americans never saw combat, but only supported the minority who did the actual fighting.

And much of that hundredweight came in the form of what to the Vietnamese seemed luxury goods. (I knew an American mother who once a week airmailed her soldier son a bar of Dial Gold soap, to quell the bacteria. He recommended the soap to others, and eventually dozens of bars of Dial arrived in the company mail room every week.) Indeed, the US eventually resorted to importing motor scooters, television sets, and refrigerators, just to soak up the dollars that were floating around, to keep inflation from going completely out of control. It's hard to believe that Cowboy didn't dip into that cornucopia, one way or another, like almost everyone else in South Vietnam.

~ ~ ~

Morris himself exploited Cowboy's recruiting skills. Tasked with reopening an abandoned Special Forces base at Bu Prang — a few kilometers inside Vietnam but almost within shouting distance of the FULRO base at Camp le Rolland — he asked Cowboy to supply him a company of Highlanders. The C Team commander naturally expected them to be untrained. When they were trucked into the Pleiku airfield, where they were to be outfitted and flown to Bu Prang, they did indeed seem as if they'd come straight from the forest. About half wore a loincloth as their only garment, while others were dressed in civilian clothes or faded army fatigues. But when they jumped off the deuce-and-a-half trucks, they formed up smartly into squads and platoons, having learned the military arts from their FULRO drill sergeants. Indeed, it's possible they'd come the wearisome 320 kilometers from Camp le Rolland, only to fly back virtually the same distance to Bu Prang.

So Cowboy had provided a battalion of Strikers for Bu Prang and another for the B-50 Mike Force near Ban Me Thuot. If he required each man to remit ten percent of his salary, the tithes for a thousand men would have amounted to a considerable sum. Presumably some of it went to support his mysterious Dam-Y Division training center, and perhaps some went back to FULRO. But some obviously had paid for his Akai tape deck, his Honda motorcycle, and that robin-egg-blue pickup truck.

By the end of 1967, Cowboy had so many balls in the air that he was in danger of dropping them. His superiors in FULRO were weary of his skimming off money that should have come to them, and the various American agencies in Saigon had likewise tired of his trickery. All that was needed was an excuse to get rid of him.

A Bullet Between the Eyes

ON THE NIGHT of December 8, 1967, Cowboy went to his favorite hangout, the Darlac II nightclub in Ban Me Thuot. His current girl-friend, a Vietnamese named Thu, was a hostess there, dancing with customers in hopes they would buy her a glass of colored water that was priced as whiskey. Cowboy got into an argument with an ARVN sergeant who was dancing with Thu. "In the heat of anger," Gerald Hickey wrote, "Philippe killed the sergeant and fled south on Route 14 to the FULRO base in the vicinity of 'Bridge 14,' some fourteen kilometers from Ban Me Thuot," a route that would have taken him past his house in Buon Ale A. Bridge 14 spans the Song Srepok.

Cowboy couldn't resist the lure of Ban Me Thuot's nightlife. One evening he went with some FULRO "Young Turks" to the International Bar downtown, accompanied by young women from a Rhade dance group. Some ARVN soldiers came into the bar, one of them asked a Rhade girl to dance, and a fight broke out. "Several of the Vietnamese were wounded," Gerald Hickey wrote, "the bar was wrecked, and Philippe again fled the town." Mike Benge adds the detail that Cowboy's weapon was a Colt .45 like the one I carried while at the Buon Beng FOB.

To smooth things over, Cowboy went into town early in January to plead his case with the province chief, Colonel Le Van Thanh. The colonel arranged for him to talk to higher-ups in Saigon. As Cowboy told the story, the discussions included Nguyen Cao Ky, the air force general and former prime minister who was now vice-president in the administration of General Nguyen Van Thieu. Apparently they asked Cowboy to assassinate Y Bham Enoul and other FULRO leaders, for which service the generals would pay him handsomely and install him in Y Bham's place as head of the independence movement.

Back in Ban Me Thout, Cowboy stayed out of sight by living at his mother's house in the village of Buon Pan Lam. However, a FULRO member known as Thomas managed to locate him and invited him to dinner. Cowboy accepted, but took the precaution of going to Thomas's house in an American jeep and accompanied by a SMIAT enlisted man who went by the name of Joe, whose presence might give him protection. Before the meal was over, however, two armed FULRO groups blocked the front and rear entrances to the house. A Rhade couple, also invited to dinner, ran for protection to a bunker outside the house; the husband was shot and badly wounded.

The wounded man happened to be Y Trong Hwing, whose brother was an officer in the B-50 Mike Force outside of town. Thinking that he was Cowboy, and that they had succeeded in their mission, the assassination squad left in a hurry. Cowboy and Joe escaped out the back, leaving the SMIAT jeep behind.

This is Mike Benge's version of the story, which I am inclined to follow because he was on the scene. Gerald Hickey, in *Free in the Forest*, has Cowboy calling the meeting in order to further a plan to assassinate the FULRO leaders. Y Trong Hwing objected, the two got into an argument, and *Cowboy* was the one who shot him. However it happened, Mike was brought into the situation in hopes that American intervention might save Y Trong's life. He arranged to have the wounded man taken to the provincial hospital in the abandoned jeep, but Y Trong died on the operating table.

Cowboy meanwhile made his way home, got his own vehicle (a jeep, Mike says), and drove out to the airfield east of town where B-50 was based. Improbable as it seems — even if he hadn't just shot an officer's kid brother — he managed to persuade some of the Mike Force troopers to join him, and in the process to steal two .30-caliber machineguns from the helicopters, a bazooka (more likely an M-79 Blooper), grenades, five cases of M-16 rifles, and a deuce-and-a-half and a three-quarter-ton in which to haul it all away. This makes more sense if, as Jim Morris wrote, the B-50 troops were indeed a rent-a-battalion from Cowboy's Dam-Y Division.

Mike Benge now drove to Buon Ale A and the FULRO office there. He managed to enlist the help of the province chief and his American advisor, while the FULRO men took off in "an assortment of motorbikes,

Vespas, Lambrettas, and Honda motorcycles" toward Buon Ea Pur, past the airport and fifteen kilometers east of town. Colonel Thanh agreed to let the FULRO convoy pass through the ARVN checkpoints, while Mike and the American advisor went to Emperor Bao Dai's former guest house, the Grand Bungalow, now quarters for the US military. There, they woke the Air Force officer commanding the Cessna L-19 Bird Dogs that provided Forward Air Control for the military in the area. They arranged for an L-19 to circle over Buon Ea Pur, starting at sunrise, with another standing by to take its place when it had to refuel.

"At dawn," Mike wrote in his memoir, "I was at district headquarters and on the radio with the FAC pilot. He reported that several jeeps and other vehicles surrounded [Buon Ea Pur] and a group on the outside seemed to be talking through the gate with a group on the inside. After a couple of hours, the gate to the village opened and a dozen or so Montagnards in [camouflage fatigues] came out and one was tied up, whom I assumed was Philippe, and loaded onto the back of a logging truck, a bunch of others also climbed on, some were armed, and it drove off back in the direction of Ban Me Thuot."

Instead of going to town, however, the truck turned south on Route 21 and drove to the village of K'ram, eight kilometers south of town. There the L-19 lost track of it. It apparently traveled through side roads to Route 14 and the FULRO post at Bridge 14, where Cowboy was shot to death. There was a cover story that a VC sniper just happened to kill him, but that was so improbable that not even the ARVN would believe it. Supposedly the sniper was so skilled that, of all the people in the party, he not only managed to single out Cowboy, but to hit him "between the eyes." This was the story as told to Mike by one of the men who had been in the escort, and who now wore Cowboy's "large tiger's eye gold ring on his finger." It was a sapphire, and a prize possession.

I like to believe that the bullet-between-the-eyes wasn't just a flourish, and that Cowboy did indeed meet a sudden and unexpected death. But he was certainly gone, the man I knew as Cowboy, whom the Americans generally called Philip, who as a teenager had styled himself Philippe Drouin, and who as a baby had been named Y Kdruin Mlo.

~ ~ ~

In *War Story*, Jim Morris tells a strange tale of how he learned of his friend's death. Called to Saigon in January 1968 to represent Special Forces in a conference about the Highlanders, he reported to the American embassy and joined a group of well-fed suits in a room-within-a-room, raised off the outside floor and sealed from all possibility of eavesdropping. "It put me in mind immediately of a bad James Bond movie," he wrote. He had worn his "rumpled cruddies" as a calculated affront to the REMFs in Saigon, and he and his companion were the only men in uniform.

The master of ceremonies turned out to be Gerald

Hickey, who had been in Vietnam off and on since the 1950s. Though paid by the Rand Corporation, a private think tank, the anthropologist's ultimate employer was the US military. "He too was a well-fed smooth civilian," in Morris's opinion, but he was willing to forgive Hickey because he had spent much time in the field, sometimes in danger of his life. "He was always quiet, always amiable, always friendly and he knew what the score was in Vietnam."

Morris then looked at the printed agenda for the meeting, which included an item that startled him: *Philippe Drouin.*

"I think, gentlemen," Hickey said, as Morris reconstructed the meeting in *War Story,* "we can cross one item off the agenda. My information is that Philippe Drouin was assassinated yesterday by political opponents within the FULRO organization. He will trouble us no more."

What sort of trouble Cowboy posed for the suits at the American embassy is not made clear in this or any other account. Certainly Dr. Hickey does not mention such a meeting in *Window on a War,* in which he surveyed his near-twenty-year acquaintance with the country.

Morris did manage to confirm some of the details of his friend's death, some time later in Ban Me Thuot. Cowboy comes out looking better in this version: it was not he but his bodyguard who shot the Vietnamese sergeant at the Darlac II; and the intramural battle between him and the FULRO leaders was

126

more of a tong war than a planned execution. And Morris was later told that Cowboy wasn't killed at Bridge 14, but had made his escape — on a bicycle! The captain liked that touch, though he conceded that Cowboy would have preferred to flee on a motorcycle.

In a FULRO bill of particulars, dated January 26, 1968, Cowboy was charged with multiple "crimes of thievery and trickery," to a value of 5,812,000 piasters — about $244,000 today. Cowboy had squandered this small fortune, the indictment said, on "his personal pleasures (dancing, eating, drinking, etc.)." That would indeed have paid for a lot of evenings with Thu at the Darlac II. More to the point, Cowboy had conspired with Vietnamese officials to murder FULRO leaders, for which betrayal of his position as a colonel in the liberation movement he had been condemned to death.

~ ~ ~

Just five days after the FULRO indictment, the Communists launched what amounted to a suicide attack on Saigon, Hue, and other population centers in South Vietnam. This was the famed "Tet Offensive," during the truce that traditionally accompanied the Lunar New Year festival. It was a disaster for both sides. For the North Vietnamese, General Giap fully believed that the South Vietnamese people would rise up and overthrow the government; instead, the Viet Cong was effectively destroyed as a fighting force, as the unprepared ARVN and the US military recovered their wits and fought back.

In the United States, however, newspaper and especially television accounts of the fighting were nothing short of hysterical, playing and replaying scenes of carnage on the grounds of the US embassy in Saigon. For the increasing number of Americans who doubted the wisdom of their country's involvement in a Vietnamese civil war, Tet seemed proof that it had all been folly.

One of the victims of Tet was Mike Benge, the USAID worker in Ban Me Thuot who was one of my resources for this book. In the confused street fighting in the night of January 28, he drove around in his jeep to collect American civilians and take them to safety. On his last trip, to the leper hospital, he was captured along with two missionaries, Betty Ann Olson and Harry Blood, both of whom died on the long march into Cambodia. After three years en route, Mike finally made it to the infamous "Hanoi Hilton" in North Vietnam.

Ban Me Thuot was a center of PAVN attack in the Tet Offensive. Many civilians died in Buon Ale A, Y Bham Enoul's home village, where the Communists also murdered five American missionaries. When the fighting ended, some four thousand Rhade sought shelter in Ban Me Thuot, their homes destroyed and their food stolen by the Communists.

Following Tet, the avuncular television personality Walter Cronkite visited South Vietnam for a special report on the war. It ended with a verdict that at the time seemed impossible to dispute: *"But it is increas-*

ingly clear to this reporter that the only rational way out then will be to negotiate, not as victors, but as an honorable people who lived up to their pledge to defend democracy, and did the best they could."

In other words, we should cut and run. I watched that CBS News special report on a black-and-white portable TV in our living room, which had formerly been a woodshed tacked on to the rear of the house. I remembered his words somewhat differently — that he said *we could* rather than *they could* — but I knew that they had changed everything. I could scarcely get my breath when he concluded: "This is Walter Cronkite. Good night."

Cut and run! That is exactly what we did, though in the nature of politics and war, we took almost as long to escape from Vietnam as we did to become entangled in it — the same six years that Mike Benge spent as a prisoner of the North Vietnamese. In this process, nobody suffered more than the Highlanders.

No Longer Free in the Forest

THE VIETNAM MEMORIAL in Washington is, I think, the finest piece of national recollection ever built. And how wonderfully apt that it was designed by a college girl of Asian parentage!

I visited the Wall early one morning in 1987, and for the first time in my life encountered art that made me weep. I started on the west, with the Lincoln Memorial behind me, so I would be walking toward morning – that seemed appropriate. I walked down a slight incline, as if descending into the earth. The first panel of names was a foot or so high, with a single line of names, but this was just the first of one hundred and forty panels, all but the last of them taller. At the lowest point – call it the perigee – the Wall stood so high above me that I could not touch the topmost name. The panel to my right covered the years 1957 to 1965.

Here I could search for the names of people I had met in Vietnam, finding two from my month in the Mekong Delta, the helicopter crewmen Ted Winowitch and Jim Wright. (Walter Swain, the executive officer at Buon Beng, was a later casualty. He was twenty-eight when he stepped on a land-mine in 1967, therefore twenty-five when I followed his crabbed gait on the march to Tan Hoa.) Also on this panel were two of the Green Berets I've had occasion to mention in this book, Terry Cordell and Bukey Brainerd.

Reading the nearly seven hundred names on that panel was like hearing an anthem of American immigration. It was tilted somewhat toward those who'd settled below the Mason-Dixon Line, since the men who went to Vietnam in the early years tended to be volunteers, and Southerners were most likely to volunteer for the military. I especially liked the fact that no ranks were shown: Captain Cordell and PFC Winowitch were equals in death.

At this point, I had already turned a corner – yes! – and could walk up toward morning again. The final panel, like the first one, remembered those who died at the midpoint of the body count, in May 1969.

Altogether, the Wall contains the names of 58,310 US servicemen and 8 women killed in Southeast Asia – soldiers, sailors, marines, airmen, and nurses. A surprising number were not combat deaths, reflecting the fact that most of those who served in Vietnam, except on rare occasions, saw combat at a distance.

~ ~ ~

Running for president in 1968, Richard Nixon promised to "end the war and win the peace." It took him a while, and indeed he first widened the war by extending it into Cambodia and Laos. At the same time, he and Henry Kissinger sent out peace feelers to Moscow, Bejing, and Hanoi, and began secret talks in Paris with the North Vietnamese. About a hundred

131

thousand American soldiers came home in 1969-1970, in the process called "Vietnamization," as the ARVN began to take back the defense of the country. Like a movie running backward, US forces left the country over the next three years, at about the same rate President Johnson had sent them there. They weren't the same individuals, of course, because of the American fixation on short tours of duty. Altogether, about three million US servicemen took part in the Vietnam War, a figure that included thirty thousand Canadians. Troops of other nations included three hundred thousand South Koreans, sixty thousand Australians, forty thousand Thai, four thousand New Zealanders, and two thousand Filipinos.

Among other reductions, the 5th Special Forces Group was shut down in 1970, and the CIDG camps and their indigenous Strikers were absorbed by the ARVN Rangers. There were thirty-seven of these "Border Ranger" battalions, about fifteen thousand men, the vast majority from Highland tribes. Thus Dave Nuttle's Civilian Irregular Defense Groups were finally conscripted into the regular army, as the Ngo brothers had wanted to do from the beginning.

In some accounts, the Border Rangers posted one of the highest desertion rates in the South Vietnamese military, which if true would not be surprising. But overall the Highlanders fought longer and harder than did the ARVN — some of them in Cambodian Army uniforms. Gerald Hickey visited Phnom Penh in 1970 and, among others, met Major Kpa Doh, the junior interpreter from Buon Beng. Y Bham Enoul was also there, though in somewhat confusing circumstances: Hickey was told that FULRO had placed Y Bham under "house arrest" for fear he might sell out the organization to the South Vietnamese government.

In 1971, Australia and New Zealand withdrew their troops from South Vietnam, and the American commitment dropped below two hundred thousand. As a test, the PAVN launched a conventional invasion across the demilitarized zone the following spring, but it was defeated by air power, and the Americans continued to go home. By the end of 1972, only seventy thousand US servicemen remained in South Vietnam; only a thousand were combat troops, and their activities were tightly controlled in order to keep casualties (and anti-war protests) to a minimum.

In January 1973, the US halted air strikes on North Vietnam, a peace agreement was signed in Paris, and Hanoi began to release the prisoners it held. Altogether, 591 came home, including Mike Benge from the USAID mission in Ban Me Thuot. He flew out of Hanoi on March 5, on a plane whose other passengers included two Filipino workers and two German nurses, one of them a woman, who had been captured by the Viet Cong. While still on medical leave, Mike returned to Saigon and USAID, one of the hundreds if not thousands of Americans — including Jim Morris and Gerald Hickey — who had become so deeply committed to the country and the cause that they could never turn their backs on it.

Not surprisingly, the longest-serving POW was a

Green Beret, Captain Floyd Thompson, captured *nine years* earlier when the Cessna L-19 Bird Dog in which he was a passenger was shot down not far from his CIDG camp in Quang Tri, near the 17th parallel that separated the two halves of Vietnam.

The last American combat troops were gone from South Vietnam by this time, but the war went on. In August 1974, beset by inflation and the Watergate scandal, President Nixon resigned to avoid an almost certain impeachment vote by Congress, which might well have resulted in his removal from office and the loss of his pension and perks. In the mid-term elections that November, the Democrats increased their Senate and House majorities, and also their determination to put an end to the fighting.

Hanoi soon tested American resolve by besieging the town of Phuoc Long, on Route 14 southwest of Ban Me Thuot. Though the ARVN fought well, Phuoc Long fell to the PAVN on January 6, 1975. Gerald Ford – the first and so far the only president never to have prevailed in a national election – pleaded for funds to resupply the South Vietnamese, but Congress denied him the money. That was, in effect, a blank check for Hanoi, which now understood that it could violate the Paris agreement without consequences. Similarly, the Communist Pathet Lao and Khmer Rouge were freed to take control of Laos and Cambodia. Though the "domino theory," advanced by President Eisenhower in 1954 to justify intervening in Vietnam, generally brings a pitying smile to the lips of college professors, it certainly worked in the former colonies of French Indochina.

The PAVN by this time had completed thousands of kilometers of all-weather roads through Laos, Cambodia, and South Vietnam, not to mention an oil pipeline, a radio network, and two corps headquarters located inside the enemy's territory. Soon after the fall of Phuoc Long, the Communists launched *Chien dich Mua Xuan 1975*, the Spring Offensive of 1975, to complete the conquest of South Vietnam. It began toward the end of February, with an artillery barrage against Pleiku. On March 3, the PAVN destroyed a Regional Force battalion and secured a 20-kilometer stretch of Highway 19, allowing it to drive its Russian-built tanks — as good as any in the world — into South Vietnam.

But it was not Pleiku but Ban Me Thuot that was their target. This was guerrilla warfare with tanks! The PAVN brought the T-54s and T-55s one hundred kilometers south, through forest and over the Song Srepok, which they bridged with a span sturdy enough to carry a thirty-five-ton burden. As the tanks approached the town overnight on March 10-11, the rattle of their treads and the roar of their diesel engines was covered by a near-continual artillery barrage, sufficient to bring them to the outlying villages before their presence was known.

In a region where battles often involved a handful of men and rarely more than a single regiment, Ban Me Thuot was invested by three full *divisions*, thirty or forty thousand men. Their first task was to cut the approaches to the town, including the FULRO outpost at Bridge 14 to the southwest. By mid-morning on March 11 the North Vietnamese 316th Division was in control of Ban Me Thuot.

Though in the Highlands overall the ARVN had a considerable edge, in this battle they were out-numbered five to one. "The puppet troops were really panicked," a North Vietnamese officer recalled in 1983. "It was total confusion. . . . They threw their guns down the wells and down outhouses. They put on civilian clothes, including clothes they stole from the inhabitants. . . . They even put on women's clothes in order to escape. . . . Their units had disintegrated and they were simply fleeing for their lives." Among those taken prisoner were the Darlac province chief and the deputy commander of the ARVN 23rd Division.

When Ban Me Thuot fell, it was as if the cork had been pulled from the bottle. Not only the town's defenders, but those in Cheo Reo, Pleiku, and even Kontum to the north began a headlong flight to the seacoast. Their losses were horrendous. Hoping to avoid a repeat of earlier disasters at the Mang Yang Pass on Highway 19, Saigon called for a withdrawal along the same rough road I had followed in 1964, along the Song Ba southeast of Cheo Reo. Tens of thousands of troops and civilians became trapped in a traffic jam on what was grandly called Interprovincial Route 7B but was, in fact, just a rough dirt road. By

Hanoi's account, which is really all we have, the ARVN in escaping from the Highlands lost fifty-eight thousand men killed, wounded, captured, missing, or (by far the largest category) deserted. PAVN casualties were about three thousand.

With the Highlands gone, the Saigon government had little more than a month to live.

~ ~ ~

In Cambodia, the Communist Khmer Rouge — led by the homicidal Pol Pot and supported by China and North Vietnam — set out to duplicate what the PAVN was doing in South Vietnam. Phnom Penh fell to the Khmer Rouge on April 16. Kpa Doh, Y Bham Enoul, and other Highlanders took refuge in the French embassy. But the French gave them up when the Communists demanded that they be turned over. They were imprisoned at Lambert Stadium, where some were executed, while others were trucked to an unknown location and never heard from again.

On April 30, Saigon fell to the PAVN. By a curious twist, the president who broadcast the surrender statement was the same General Duong Van Minh who had briefly ruled South Vietnam after the overthrow of Ngo Dinh Diem in 1963. This time, "Big Minh" held his office for just two days.

The photos of people being rescued by helicopters from the roof of the American embassy have become so much a part of the Vietnam War story that many or most westerners believe that the US Army was actually defeated by the PAVN, though all American combat troops had left the country two years earlier. It was the ARVN that collapsed, and that only after the collapse of America's will to supply them.

Few if any Highlanders were rescued in the airlift and sealift that brought out the last Americans and thousands of Vietnamese who had worked with them. Edmund Sprague, a former Green Beret noncom who had returned to South Vietnam to work with the Highlanders, arranged for several hundred to assemble on a beach in Nha Trang to board an American ship, but it never turned up. Nay Luett, from his position as head of the Ministry for Development of Ethnic Minorities in Saigon, got others to presumed safety on Phu Quoc Island off the southern coast, but apparently they weren't rescued either. The Ministry was abolished in June, and Nay Luett, Paul Nur, and others were put in a "reeducation camp" by the victorious Communists, under awful conditions. Some died, and others were executed; a few survived and eventually made their way to the United States.

The horrors that followed the Communist victory were like those that befell Hue during the 1967 Tet Offensive, only on a country-wide scale. Dave Nuttle tells what happened to the Jarai family whose fate had become entangled with his, and with Cowboy's: "In May 1975, a Communist police unit, under the direction of a Captain Pham, entered H'un's village and shot her and her father, Nay Moul, for working with the Americans. Several of H'un's relatives were taken to prison, and Marina (then age 15) was hit over the head, by Pham, with the butt of his rifle. Marina was left for dead.... As fate would have it, [the girl] was saved and healed by her grandmother, who kept Marina hidden and cared for in a secret room in her house, for the next 14 months."

Gerald Hickey estimated at least 200,000 and perhaps as many as 220,000 Highlanders died as a result of the Vietnam War, as soldiers or as civilians; and that perhaps 85 percent of their villages were destroyed or abandoned. The new government made no effort to repair the damage. Indeed, the Communists adopted and accelerated Ngo Dinh Diem's policy of settling ethnic Vietnamese in the Highlands. By 1988, some four hundred thousand lowlanders had moved into Darlac province alone, vastly outnumbering the indigenous population.

The Highlanders were forced to move out of their longhouses (which besides being part of their heritage also served to keep the family away from the low-flying mosquitoes that carried the malaria parasite) into conventional dwellings. Housing was forcibly intermingled, breaking up the tribal, clan, and family relationships that had once marked Highland villages. The Communists banned swidden agriculture, whereby a family would burn off a plot of field or forest, farm it for a few years, then let it recover for ten years or so. Their religious practices were also banned, both animist and Christian. The object, as the Communists explained, was to "turn nomads into sedentary workers" in state farms and logging camps, to abolish "backward customs and habits," and to "join the advance to socialism." (How often have we heard that last phrase as a cover for atrocity!) On the internet, reports are common though unverified that rape, forced marriage, and abortion were also used to "Vietnamize" the Highlanders.

And the forests were clear-cut for lumber — damage more lasting than the Agent Orange used as a defoliant during the war. "Communist policy," Hickey concluded in *Shattered World* in 1993, "casts a shadow not only on the Highland world but also on the mountain environment and the ultimate fate of Vietnamese settlers."

The new century has not brought much relief. On two occasions, Highlanders demonstrated against government repression, only to meet even more repression. "Government security forces blocked key bridges and intersections," reported Human Rights Watch in 2006. "When the demonstrators refused to turn back, police fired tear gas, beating people who were seated or when they fell down. Suspected organizers of the protests were dragged away and arrested. Afterwards, the police entered the villages, ransacking houses and beating villagers as they searched for activists. By Easter evening [2004], the provincial hospitals were full of wounded highlanders, bloody from cracked skulls and broken arms and legs. At least ten highlanders were killed." The organization published the names of 355 Highlanders imprisoned for such crimes as "undermining national unity" and "organizing illegal migrations." Most of the names seem to be those of the Rhade and Jarai tribes.

~ ~ ~

Long after the fall of Saigon, FULRO fought on. Highlanders armed themselves from the great heaps of weapons abandoned by the ARVN in their flight before the advancing North Vietnamese, and they took to the forest or fled across the border to Cambodia and Laos. Their numbers were estimated at ten thousand in 1975, dropping to two thousand by the end of the decade. In 1984, several hundred insurgents gave up the fight and headed west to Thailand, where they arrived a year later, having walked a thousand kilometers while living off the land. Two hundred were brought to the United States in November 1986.

Another band, more persistent or perhaps more lucky, settled in Mondulkiri province, a wilderness the size of the state of New York. (Phumi Dak Dam, once called Camp le Rolland, is on the southeastern edge of this vast tract, fifteen kilometers by road from the Vietnam border.) In August 1992, freelance journalist Nate Thayer visited their camps. "Based in a string of five riverine villages carved out of dense forest," he wrote in *Far Eastern Economic Review*, "the guerrillas have no access to any commodities except the small gifts fighters bring back from their raids into Vietnam. There are no medicines, and many of the soldiers and their families possess only weapons and clothes."

Thayer talked to the leader, Colonel Y Peng Ayun, an ailing, bespectacled fifty-year-old Rhade who said he had been fighting for twenty-eight years — i.e., since the FULRO rebellion of 1964. He claimed four hundred followers, a figure that apparently included their families. They survived as hunter-gatherers, with small gardens to raise corn, pumpkins, cucumbers, and peppers. The headquarters group fell silent or wept when Thayer told them that Y Bham Enoul had been murdered by the Khmer Rouge seventeen years before.

After an appeal from Pierre K'Briuh, one of the Highlanders living in North Carolina, 398 FULRO diehards surrendered to Uruguayan soldiers of a UN peacekeeping force on October 10, 1992. The guerrillas turned over their flag, along with 194 weapons — just enough to outfit a single rifle company — and 2,567 rounds of ammunition, which a ten-man US Army squad would have burned up in a ten-minute firefight. In addition to "aged but immaculately-maintained" rifles, there was a single M-79 "Blooper" with one grenade.

In total, perhaps a thousand Highlanders made their way to the United States over the years. Many of them settled in the vicinity of Fort Bragg, North Carolina, to be near the Green Berets who had trained and supported them twenty or thirty years before. Their community now numbers about four thousand. Among them is Cowboy's younger half-brother, Ysang Yap Mlo. Most of them came from refugee camps in

Cambodia and Thailand, and a few were rescued from Vietnam itself, usually by paying an exorbitant "exit fee." Thus, in 1990, Dave Nuttle was able to learn that his daughter Marina was still alive, and to bring her and her family to the United States.

"The Montagnard people and the Americans are like one family," one of the FULRO diehards told Nate Thayer in 1992. "I am not angry, but very sad that the Americans forgot us. The Americans are like our elder brother, so it is very sad when your brother forgets you." He might have been speaking for a million fellow Highlanders, and indeed for the many millions of South Vietnamese who did not want to live under Hanoi's rule.

How the Work Was Done

THE VIETNAMESE put their family name first but almost always address one another by their last or personal name, thus President Diem and his brother Nhu, both of the Ngo family. An exception is Ho Chi Minh, known as "Uncle Ho" to his followers.

I spell Vietnamese words the way they usually appeared in the 1960s, and with no diacritical marks. The most significant name changes have been to Saigon, now Ho Chi Minh City; to Cheo Reo, now Ayun Pa; and to the province of Darlac, now Dak Lak. (Both Cheo Reo and Darlac were French corruptions of indigenous names.) David Nuttle renders his wife's name as Rcom H'unh, and he ought to know, but I go along with the published histories, notably the books by Gerald Hickey and Paul Harris. Throughout, I avoid using all capital letters in Mike Force and Rand Corporation, even when quoting others. Cowboy's American friends sometimes spelled "Philip" with a double *l*, sometimes with one; I have similarly harmonized the spelling throughout.

Perhaps inconsistently, I avoid the 1954-1975 term "Central Highlands." After the Communist victory, the adjective was dropped because the Highlands are no longer central to the unified country, and that seems perfectly logical to me.

With the refreshing exception of the CIA, American nomenclature in Vietnam was in a continual state of change in the 1960s. I have glossed over some of these changes. For example, USAID was still called USOM (US Operating Mission) when I was in the country. And I have written "US military" rather than get tangled up with MAAG (Military Assistance Advisory Group, 1950-1964) and MACV (Military Assistance Command, Vietnam, 1962-1973).

Like the "Montagnards" as a people, the "Rhade" were named by the French, and the word is pronounced more or less as "rah-*day*." Their own favored name is Ede, also pronounced as two syllables. The characterization of Nay Luett is from John Prados, *Hidden History*, and his language ability was confirmed by Mike Benge. For the Highlanders' history and lifestyle, I rely mostly on Gerald Hickey, especially his *Sons of the Mountains*. The text in that book (page 335) conflicts with the chart at the back, making it difficult to sort out the Rcom family relationships.

The Buon Enao project is likewise a challenge. Each of the principals — David Nuttle, Paul Campbell, and Ronald Shackleton — understandably focuses on his own role to the exclusion of others. This distortion is especially significant in the case of Capt. Shackleton, who arrived in 1962 and therefore had nothing to do with its origins; unfortunately, his version was the first to be published and remains the one accepted by US Army historians. And of course many others contributed to the project besides those named in the text, both American and Vietnamese.

Capt. Arritola's team was originally A-35, but the numbering system was changed while they were in Vietnam. Of the rest of the detachment, Capt. Herman Durrwachter died on January 13, 1962, in what was apparently a non-combat accident. Sergeant Wayne Marchand and Specialist James Gabriel were murdered by their Viet Cong captors on April 8 because they were too badly wounded to keep up with the guerrillas. (Their names too can be found on Panel 1E of the Vietnam Wall.)

The Royal Navy "Q-ships" were named for their base at Queenstown (now Cobh) in Ireland, then a part of the United Kingdom.

To summarize the structure of the Buon Enao Strike Force, there were 12 men in a squad, two squads or 24 men in a platoon, and five platoons or 120 men in each company. When it comes to the VIP tourists at Buon Enao, I can find no mention of General Krulak or Secretary McNamara visiting South Vietnam before 1963.

At a time when an A Team routinely had two captains, Lieutenant McFadden was an outlier. I suspect he was sent to Vietnam as the detachment's executive officer. One of Steve Sherman's documents shows a Capt. Leon Hope assigned to A-223, then "dropped"; presumably he was one of the Green Berets sent home by Dave Nuttle. The camp at Buon Tha is variously identified as Buon Tan Mo and Buon

Tha Mo, and its exact location is a mystery. Similarly, the "Cu Ken mountains" defy identification today.

The twin-engine B-26 of Vietnam was a modified Douglas A-26 attack plane of the Second World War, though it confusingly bore the same designation as that conflict's Martin B-26 medium bomber. Capt. Cordell is often cited as the first Green Beret officer killed in action in Vietnam, though that dubious honor belongs to Harry Cramer (see below).

For the fascinating story of the 1963 coup, see chapter 8, "Getting rid of Diem," in Stanley Karnow's admirable history of Vietnam.

Cowboy's letter of introduction appears in full, and with identical phrasing, in Jim Morris's 1979 book and in Johnnie Corns's 2009 memoir. I doubt they both kept a copy for posterity. More likely, Morris reconstructed it from memory, and General Corns adopted that version. To judge by his name tag at Buon Beng, Cowboy had indeed Americanized his first name as *Philip*.

Parts of chapters 7, 8, and 10 are adapted from my Vietnam journal, *The Only War We've Got*. When we watched the occupation of Iraq as a reality show on television, I realized that for the US Army of 2003, a Forward Operating Base was an installation equipped with a store, a cinema, air-conditioned offices, wi-fi, and probably a McDonald's restaurant. Not so in the 1960s. The Song Ba has since been dammed, so I cannot locate the FOB, but I think it was near the present hamlet of Cau Le Bac. I am enchanted to see that Route 7, the rough road I traveled to get there, is now celebrated as part of the historic *Truong Son Dong*, Strategic Supply Route, as the Vietnamese remember what we called the Ho Chi Minh Trail.

GI Gin was a robust mixture of terpin hydrate, an expectorant; 110-proof alcohol; and codeine. Alas, the US military phased it out in the 1980s. The January 1954 ambush of Group Mobile 100 to the east of Cheo Reo (Route 7) was a foretaste of its disaster five months later at the Mang Yang Pass (Highway 19). Interestingly, the regimental elite were the men of the *Bataillon de Corée* who had fought alongside American troops in Korea, and who still wore the Indian Head patch of the US 2nd Infantry Division.

I'll always be grateful for the friendship of Russ Brooks and Mike Holland when I trekked with them to Tan Hoa, and for their emails when I revised my Vietnam journal for publication thirty-six years later. The John McPhee quote is from *Draft No. 4: On the Writing Process*, Farrar, Straus and Giroux, 2017.

I have not been able to identify Sergeants Baier and Caldwell from the Nha Trang Mike Force. Mike Benge thinks that the fortified village of the "Dam-Y Division" might have been the Dam San training center near Ea Kmat, site of the agricultural experiment station where Dave Nuttle had worked in 1960, and about 15 kilometers east of Ban Me Thuot.

After the Second World War, the onetime *Deuxième Bureau* became the *Service de Documentation Extérieure et de Contre-Espionnage*, Foreign Documentation and Counter-Espionage Service. The older and shorter name was regularly used in Vietnam. Despite the many maps of Ban Me Thuot, from the long years of American involvement, I cannot trace Cowboy's movements in January 1968 in any great detail. Nobody seems to know, for example, where his mother's village Buon Pan Lam was located, and many old names of tribal villages appear to have been altered to Vietnamese ones. Route 14 is shown on Google Maps as AH 17, but the old designation can be seen on Google Earth. Both the FULRO office in Buon Ale A and the outpost at Bridge 14 are on this road, which leads southwest 89 kilometers to the Cambodia border near Phui Dak Dam (Camp le Rolland) before zigzagging south in the general direction of Saigon.

Mostly I have followed Mike Benge's narrative for Cowboy's final days, "Cowboy, the Montagnards' Al Capone." However, "an assortment of motorbikes" etc. is from Hickey, *Free in the Forest*. Hickey makes no mention of the meeting described by Jim Morris.

Harry Cramer's name was added to the Vietnam Veterans' Memorial soon after it was opened to the public. He was killed by a Viet Cong mortar shell, though for political reasons his death was attributed to an "accidental explosion." Capt. Cramer remains the earliest known combat death, though in 1999 recognition was granted to an earlier serviceman, shot by an inebriated acquaintance with whom he had quarreled. Because of Ms Lin's inside-out numbering, this panel is 1E, and it contains the names of all the fatalities mentioned in this book except that of Capt. Swain, on panel 18E.

The account of the death of Rcom H'un and Nay Moul, and Marina's survival, is adapted from Dave Nuttle, "Consummate Warrior," 2017. I have changed the capitalization and spelling, to be consistent with earlier references in this book.

For what I have written, I leaned especially on the sources listed below – *Daniel Ford, April 2018*

~ ~ ~

Ahern, Thomas, *Vietnam Declassified: The CIA and Counterinsurgency*, University Press of Kentucky 2010.

Benge, Michael, "The Montagnard Revolt," in Robert Turner et al, *Indochina in the Year of the Dragon – 1964*, Radix Press 2014. "Cowboy, the Montagnards' Al Capone," a chapter in a larger memoir, dated 2015 (seen 2018). Telephone interview and emails 2017, 2018. Mike was by turns an IVS volunteer, USAID worker, and captive of the North Vietnamese, after which he returned to South Vietnam and USAID.

Brooks, Russell, emails to author 2000.

Cao Van Vien, *The Final Collapse*, Center for Military History 1983.

Colby, William, *Lost Victory: A Firsthand Account of America's Sixteen-year Involvement in Vietnam*, Contemporary Books 1989.

Corns, John, *Our Time in Vietnam*, iUniverse 2009.

Fall, Bernard, *Street Without Joy*, Pall Mall Press 1961. The classic account of the French travails in what they called "Indochina."

Fields, Arthur et al, "Buon Enao Project" on the glanmore.org website, undated (seen 2017).

Ford, Daniel, *Incident at Muc Wa* Doubleday 1967, Warbird Books 2012. *The Only War We've Got: Early Days in South Vietnam*, Warbird Books 2012. The latter is my Vietnam journal.

"H.", Donald, "Mike Force: An Element of Impact," on gather.com website, 2009 (seen 2018).

Harris, J.P., "The Buon Enao Experiment and American Counterinsurgency," Sandhurst Occasional Papers No 13, Royal Military Academy Sandhurst 2013. *Vietnam's High Ground: Armed Struggle for the Central Highlands, 1954-1965*, University Press of Kansas 2016 – one of the best combat histories I have ever read. Emails to author 2017.

Hickey, Gerald, *Sons of the Mountains: Ethnohistory of the Vietnamese Central Highlands to 1954* and *Free in the Forest: Ethnohistory of the Vietnamese Central Highlands, 1954-1976*, both from Yale University Press 1982. *Shattered World: Adaptation and Survival among Vietnam's Highland Peoples during the Vietnam War*, University of Pennsylvania Press 1993. *Window on a War: An Anthropologist in the Vietnam Conflict*, Texas Tech University Press 2002.

Holland, Michael, "Buon Beng – A1/433 – Mike Holland's Slides," undated PDF (seen 2018). Emails to the author 2000, 2018.

Human Rights Watch, *Repression of Montagnards: Conflicts over Land and Religion in Vietnam's Central Highlands*, 2002. *No Sanctuary: Ongoing Threats to Indigenous Montagnards in Vietnam's Central Highlands*, 2006. Both documents are online at the hrw.org website (seen 2018).

Karnow, Stanley, *Vietnam: A History*, Viking 1983. Still an essential account of the country and its tormented history, and the PBS series based on it is more trustworthy than the 2017 series from Ken Burns.

Kelly, Francis, *U.S. Army Special Forces, 1961-1971*, Department of the Army 1973.

Krejci, George, "List of Special Forces camps," online, undated (seen 2017).

Markham, James, "Hill People in Vietnam Battle to Keep Land," *NY Times* 23 Oct 1973.

McCulloch, William Crews, "Philippe Drouin aka Cowboy," typescript 2017. Emails to author 2017.

Morris, Jim, *War Story*, Dell 1985 – a wonderful combat memoir. Telephone interview and emails to author 2017, 2018.

Ngo Minh Kha, interview on *Vietnam: A Television History* 1983, online at wgbh.org (seen 2018).

Nuttle, David, "They Have Stone Ears, Don't They?" undated typescript. "Consummate Warrior," chapter from a larger memoir 2017. Telephone interview and emails to author 2017, 2018. Dave sent me two versions of his memoir; I have quoted from both.

Phillips, David, "Going Local: Operation Switchback in Vietnam," Rand Corporation online 29 Aug 2015.

Piasecki, Eugene, "Civilian Irregular Defense Group: The First Years, 1961-1967," *Veritas: Journal of Army Special Operations History*, online 2009 (seen 2017).

Prados, John, *The Hidden History of the Vietnam War*, Ivan R. Dee 1995.

Shackleton, Ronald, *Village Defense: Initial Special Forces Operations in Vietnam*, Phoenix Press 1975. A somewhat myopic view that has colored most US military accounts ever since.

"Special Forces Heraldry," online at the sfahq.com website, undated (seen 2017).

Sherman, Stephen, *Who's Who from 1st SFG (A) in Vietnam*, Radix Press 1995. Editor, *"Broken Promise," by Seth Adam Gitell; "Betrayal as Usual," by Jim Morris; and Other Readings about U.S. Army Special Forces and the Montagnards of South Vietnam*, Radix Press 2012. *Who's Who from 7th Special Forces Group TDY in RVN*, Radix Press 2013. Telephone interview, emails, and documents 2017, 2018. When it comes to the Green Berets, Steve Sherman is the equivalent of the National Archives.

Thayer, Nate, "The Forgotten Army" and "Trail of Tears" in *Far Eastern Economic Review* 19 Sep 1992. With Leo Dobbs, "Tribal Fighters Head for Refuge in USA" in *Phnom Penh Post* 23 Oct 1992.

Vietnam Veterans Memorial, online at virtualwall.org (seen 2018). Even the website makes my eyes water.

Wilson, James, *Landing Zones: Southern Veterans Remember Vietnam*, Duke University Press 1990. The first chapter is an interview with Edward Bridges of A-113, Capt. Shackleton's team at Buon Enao.

Made in the USA
Monee, IL
18 May 2021